Success from Setbacks

Success
from
Setbacks

Gael Lindenfield

Thorsons

Thorsons
An Imprint of HarperCollins*Publishers*
77–85 Fulham Palace Road,
Hammersmith, London W6 8JB

First published by Thorsons 1999
This revised edition published 2000
10 9 8 7 6 5 4 3 2

A catalogue record for this book
is available from the British Library

ISBN 0 00 710037 X

Printed and bound in Great Britain by
Martins the Printers Ltd, Berwick upon Tweed

Contents

Dedication

I dedicate this book to the town and inhabitants of
    La Puebla de los Infantes
    Andalucia, Spain
    Over the last ten years, you have helped me, my family, and our many guests heal from innumerable setbacks. We have brought our bruised bodies and battered souls to your haven and always left comforted and inspired. Thank you from us all.

Acknowledgements

At the end of all the acknowledgements I have written for my earlier books, you will find one for my husband Stuart. This time I want to thank him first because he is and always has been the greatest source of support during all my years of professional writing. Not only does he spend many hours of his precious free time editing my ungrammatical scripts, he is always willing and able to help me recover my optimism and energy when they have been depleted by a setback. But for this particular book, he did even more! He spent hours on the Internet and in libraries during our Christmas break helping me to do research.

Many thanks again are due to my publishing team at Thorsons who have worked at breakneck speed to ensure that my late manuscript met its publication deadline.

I would also like to acknowledge my gratitude to the people whose inspiring stories I have recorded in this book. Reading their biographies and autobiographies strengthened my own resolve to find a practical way of helping others make a success from their setbacks.

Finally, I must acknowledge the role of my dog Basil. During the lonely hours of writing this book, he has continually refreshed my spirit with his playfulness and enthusiasm for energizing walks along the beach – whatever the weather!

About

the Author

Gael Lindenfield is a personal development trainer working with a wide range of organizations from charities to multinational businesses. She trained and worked originally as a psychiatric social worker and psychotherapist but as her career progressed, she became increasingly interested in developing self-help techniques which can be effectively used to strengthen mental health and emotional well-being.

Gael initiated and led many pioneering projects for both the statutory and voluntary mental health organizations. Later, through her writing and work with the media, she has succeeded in making her ideas and techniques available to millions of people throughout the world.

In her own personal life, Gael has also overcome many difficulties. She had a disturbed and often traumatic childhood, most of which was spent in a series of children's homes. In her adult life she has overcome many serious problems including recurring severe depressive illnesses, a divorce and the accidental death of one of her daughters, Laura, at the age of 19 years.

She now lives with her husband Stuart in Oxford. Further details on her work can be obtained from her website:

www.gael-lindenfield.com

Introduction

When asked by a friend what was to be my next book and I replied, 'Success from Setbacks', she answered: *'Oh, you mean the story of your life.'*

I can remember feeling a bit taken aback and lost for words, although I did hear my 'automatic pilot' come out with a polite, ineffectual response. The remark haunted me for some time as I pondered on whether or not it was true. Certainly, I have a history of overcoming many (but *not* all!) challenges in my life, but the uncomfortable part of my introspection was to do with the present. At that time I knew that I was far from the point of being able to say that I was making a success out of the worst series of setbacks which I had ever experienced.

But I eventually I stopped worrying and started writing. After all, I thought, the book could help me!

In the introduction to my last book, *Emotional Confidence*, I related how on the morning after my 19-year-old daughter, Laura, died in a car crash three years ago, I was taunted by an inner voice which said:

'Now let's see what your fancy ideas can do about this, then.'

But what I didn't add in that introduction was that within the following 24 hours I also heard two other 'voices' surfacing from my unconscious mind. These were of a very different nature. The tone of the first was calm and comforting. It said:

'Your whole life has been a preparation for this.'

The second, which also surfaced apparently out of the blue, came a few hours later. Its tone was authoritative and matter-of-fact. It said:

'Laura's death is a gift. You have a choice. You can either throw it away, or you can use it.'

The messages from these voices made no sense to me at the time. Even though they were positive, I dismissed them as being cruelly incongruous in the light of our tragedy, and saw them as a sign that I was probably going insane. This was, after all, the outcome I had predicted, should such a nightmare ever become my reality.

But later, their wisdom (or should I say *my* inner wisdom?) became a lifeline and was the initial motivating force behind this book. I now know in my conscious mind that it is my *past* experience of setbacks which is helping me now, and I have already seen much evidence of the way Laura's death has been an empowering 'gift' to many, many people including myself.

And yes, I was right to start writing *before* overcoming my misgivings about my credibility. It has been a brilliant refresher exercise for me. Putting together all the insights which I had gained so far from both my personal and professional life restored my faith in my own ability to create success out of any setback. I have also been wonderfully inspired and remotivated by reading about the remarkable success so many other people have made out of a wide variety of challenges life has thrown at them.

I am well aware that I am *still* working hard to make a success out of my recent setbacks. I don't know if I'll ever reach the destination I have set for myself, but I do know that I am able to enjoy the adventurous journey once again.

The 'Theory' Behind This Book

This is quite simple. It is:

If we make a habit of making a success out of minor setbacks, we will become much more able to thrive after we have encountered a major one.

You will note that I have put quotation marks around the word 'theory'. This is because I cannot give you scientific proof of this hypothesis. It has been deduced from personal reflection, not just on my own personal experiences, but also those of many other people who have consistently risen to overcome difficult challenges in their lives.

But, of course, if you have read any of my other books, I hope you will have guessed that the main purpose of this one is not to expound a theory. It is, like my others, a *self-help programme* and its main aim is to offer some *practical* advice on how to cope constructively with setbacks.

An Overview of the Book

You will notice that I have used metaphors throughout the book.

I often ask you to imagine while you are reading that you are a cyclist on a journey. In the first chapter you will be preparing your *Kitbag*. This will contain *the seven key personal qualities of a* **Thriver**. This is the term which I use to describe **the kind of person who doesn't just** survive **after a setback, but is able to** turn it around **and use it to help create success.** There is an explanation of why we need each of these qualities, and later a self-help programme to start you off on the road to strengthening them.

In the second and third chapters you will begin to overhaul your bike! In order to support your strengthened personality, I believe you will need two exceptionally sturdy wheels:

- *Wheel 1* represents the personal skills which we need in order to be able to thrive through setbacks. You will learn how you can strengthen your *emotional, communication and organizational skills.*
- *Wheel 2* represents the areas of fitness which we need to work on. It contains a series of checklists and many suggestions to enable you to develop your own *fitness programmes for your body, mind and spirit.*
- In Chapter 4 there are exercises to help you choose your destination (*your life dream and goals*) and also plan your route (*your lifestyle.*) It also contains a short section on preparing an SOS kit for yourself (*a practical list of people you could contact in emergencies should you meet a sudden setback*).
- In Chapter 5 we will be looking at minor setbacks. You will learn how to use a new strategy which I have devised to help you develop the *Thriver habits in everyday life.*
- In Chapter 6 we will be using the metaphor of an admission to hospital after a serious accident to guide us through *recovery from a major setback.*
- In Chapter 7 I have offered some suggestions on how we can *help other people,* such as our friends, colleagues and children, make a success out of setbacks.
- In Chapter 8 you will find a *collection of relevant strategies and guidelines.* I hope these will prove to be very useful when you start putting the other seven chapters into real-life practice.
- Finally there is a short booklist which includes a guide to my earlier books, which contain many other suggestions and strategies which could help you either to become or remain a Thriver.

Throughout the text you will find that I have inserted some *quotes* which I hope you will find encouraging. I have also included a collection of *inspiring stories.* I hope you will dip into the book and read these whenever you feel in need of an injection of courage.

Have a good journey!

CHAPTER 1

Checking Your Quality Kitbag

> There are two ways of meeting difficulties: you alter the difficulties or you alter yourself to meet them.
>
> PHYLLIS BOTTOME

So what makes the personality of a Thriver so different from the average survivor?

I believe the secret lies in a combination of certain key personal qualities. It is the strength and interplay of these attributes which enable Thrivers to bounce back from all manner of difficulties. Although these qualities are most evident in times of crisis, you can also spot them in people's everyday behaviour. This is why they can *habitually* deal successfully with minor setbacks and, as a result, toughen up their personality. When the major challenge arrives they will therefore automatically respond constructively and recover quickly because they are psychologically prepared and have developed winning habits.

As I wrote in the Introduction, I have summarized these qualities under seven headings, using the word Thriver as a mnemonic to help us commit them to memory.

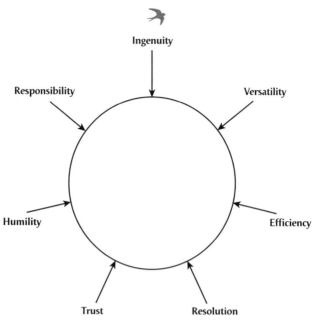

The Seven Qualities of a Thriver

Trusting
Humble
Responsible
Ingenious
Versatile
Efficient
Resolute

I appreciate that some or all of the words in my mnemonic may hold different meanings for you than they do for me. So let me first give you some of the key characteristics of each quality. I will also include some examples of the kind of behaviour we might notice in everyday life situations.

Before you start reading my list, take a moment or two to think of two or three people whom you know have success-fully battled with a number of setbacks. As you read, search your memory to find examples of when you have seen or heard about your personal examples putting these characteristics in action. This exercise is important because these examples will help to fix these qualities more firmly in the forefront of your mind where they need to be while you are working to develop them. Secondly, we all know that seeing with our own eyes is always the best way (if not the only way!) to establish belief.

TRUSTING

Thrivers are people who, first and foremost, have a *positive* outlook. For example, however bad their current situation is, they trust that:

- some good can almost always be salvaged from the worst experiences. (It is unlikely that you would hear them using despairing 'no-hope' language.)
- if a few people have let them down, they do not jump to the conclusion that everyone else in the world would also do so. (You wouldn't hear them using phrases like 'It's a dog-eat-dog world – you can't trust *anyone* these days.')
- both they themselves and others can learn from mistakes and therefore increase the chances that they will not occur again. (You wouldn't hear them beating themselves with guilt or throwing salt into other people's wounds after a mistake has been made, instead they will analyse what the experience has taught them.)
- if one aspect of a person's character proves to be 'false' or inconsistent, this does not mean that their whole character should be mistrusted. They would criticize the *specific* aspect of the person's behaviour while at the same time making it clear that they have not lost trust in that person's potential or other qualities. (You wouldn't hear them say 'You're hopeless,' but rather 'You let me down badly last week. I know that you have the best intentions and do care, but I need to ...')

> Thrivers believe that the sun will shine again one day!

- people can change and develop their personality. They would be forgiving on receipt of a sincere apology and commitment to some personal development work. (You might hear them arguing the case for giving someone a second, or even third, chance.)

HUMBLE

Thrivers are people who have a *realistic* view of themselves. Even though they generally can maintain high self-esteem, they know that:

- even though they constantly try their very best, they will inevitably fail or make mistakes at some point in their lives.
- they have many weaknesses. (You have probably heard them naming these openly and freely.)
- their strengths can sometimes fail them. (They sometimes warn you of this possibility.)
- they are capable of transgressing even their own moral code. (And will openly express their guilt when they have made a mistake or done something wrong.)
- they must ask for feedback from other people to help them assess when they may be going wrong. (They might ask 'What do you think I did well?' or 'What do you think I could have done differently?')
- many other people have desirable qualities which they do not themselves possess. (They are not afraid of envy!)
- they will manage to live much more easily and happily if they regularly ask others for support. (When they want or need help, they ask for it and do not struggle along until they can't cope on their own any longer.)

> Thrivers are human!

4

- when working in a team, their contribution, however significant, can only earn part of the credit. (They openly express their appreciation of others and their dependence on them.)

RESPONSIBLE

Thrivers take responsibility for themselves and their lives. Even though they may be aware that they have not personally caused some of the setbacks and problems they meet, they assume that it is their job to initiate and supervise *their own welfare and recovery*. So they would be the kind of people:

- whose moans and groans are short-lived. (You would see them quickly getting into action.)
- who look after their bodies and do not allow themselves to become physically debilitated by problems. (They do not suffer from a stream of endless preventable minor ailments.)
- who do not blame other people for their emotional state, even though someone else's behaviour may have triggered a feeling response. (They use language which shows that they accept that they have power over the intensity of their feelings.)
- who do not cover up their own mistakes. (They acknowledge these assertively, even though they may not broadcast them to the whole world!)
- who do not wait for others to sort out collective problems which have been brought about by a blow from 'fate' or other outside force. (So when the train is running late, *they* are probably the ones demanding to know the reason why and the anticipated time of arrival.)

> Thrivers are rocks you can depend on.

INGENIOUS

Thrivers are the kind of people you can depend on to *find new ways round seemingly impossible problems.* This is because they:

- are interested in creative approaches to problem-solving. They are not just content to take the tried-and-tested paths. (You would notice that they are always keen to explore new angles and ideas, however odd they may seem at first. This means that even though they may celebrate and appreciate the past, they generally show much more interest in the present and the future.)
- Keep their imaginations fertile by constantly conjuring up new pictures in their mind's eye. (You may often see them daydreaming or looking 'lost in their own world' when they are given a problem to solve.)
- are practical and pragmatic. (You wouldn't hear them implying that a task is too 'beneath them' to do. You might describe them as very down-to-earth even if they have exalted positions at work or in society in general.)
- take an interest in how things work. (They might drive you mad sometimes with their questions! Even if they cannot understand, they would probably show that they wish they could.)
- take an interest in the way other people may do things – especially if their way is different. (You might find them looking over your shoulder!)
- keep their brain constantly challenged by exercising and stretching it. (You wouldn't be surprised to see them doing the crossword or listening to a language tape if you bumped into them in the airport queue.)
- love an argument and encourage opposition to their ideas. (You might want to join another queue if you were at the airport and hoping for a peaceful holiday!)

Thrivers are imaginative, creative thinkers!

VERSATILE

Thrivers are *multifaceted* people and the challenge of a setback often appears to bring out another useful 'side' of them which may never have been seen before.

This is because they are people who:

- are prepared to try their hand at almost anything should the need arise. (If you were stranded on a desert island with them they would probably build the straw hut as well as learn the native language and fish for the food. You might enviously describe them as 'good all-rounders'.)
- enjoy trying out new sensations. (You would notice that they are always willing to taste new food, hear a different kind of music and try a different kind of holiday.)
- regularly adapt their style of behaviour to suit different cultures, occasions and groups of people. (You would notice that they take care to dress appropriately and adopt the manners and rituals of whoever was hosting them.)
- do not like to get stuck in ruts and will seek out change if they are becoming stale or bored. (You might find yourself having to adapt your files to keep up with their changing addresses or job titles.)
- adapt to change willingly and easily, even though they may show some resistance at the outset (I said they were human!).
- are happy to say they have changed their mind, and do not feel compelled to stick to doing something just because they have started it or said they would do it a certain way. Equally, they give others the right to do the same even if they are upset or (sometimes!) inconvenienced. (You wouldn't mind ringing them to say that you had changed your mind about something, because they might have done the same to you last week!)

> Thrivers are 'jacks of all trades' and masters of setbacks!

EFFICIENT

The Thriver is *not* someone who 'muddles through' problematic times. They are well *organized* and capable of functioning competently amid the chaos that setbacks usually set in motion because they:

- have good self-knowledge and are, therefore, able to 'play' their strengths and avoid being let down by their weaknesses. (They would be likely to be very clear about what they can or couldn't do, and you would rarely be disappointed by them.)
- 'look before they leap'. (Unless the situation is an emergency, you would notice they take time out to think carefully through the options before taking action.)
- routinely set *achievable* objectives and goals and don't make a habit of setting themselves up for failure. (They are not big gamblers, and if they did any dieting it would be short, sweet and successful!)
- work methodically. (They'd probably have an action plan for the ironing as well!)
- closely monitor their own progress. (You wouldn't need to point out to them that they were failing at a 'pet project'. They'd have noticed themselves and stopped before you summoned up the courage to tell them.)
- keep a close eye on their use of resources such as money, materials and time, and ensure that these are being used cost-effectively. (They would not overspend their budget.)
- resist being 'knee-jerked' into action by their own emotions such as fear or guilt. (They would be calm and cool when making a decision.)
- assert themselves against others who are pushing them into over-hasty action. (They will tell you if they are not yet ready to act, even though they may not want to disappoint or delay you.)

> Thrivers are not bumblers and bunglers, they are effective!

RESOLUTE

Thrivers are *determined* people. Once they have resolved to find a way forward, you know they will. They are able to do this because they:

- have high self-regard and believe that they deserve to thrive. (You do not hear them putting themselves down.)
- can assertively negotiate for what they need and want. (You know that they can drive a hard bargain.)
- are supported by their own strong moral code. (You won't see them dithering over what is the right or wrong thing to do.)
- have the courage to fight to win when necessary. (You wouldn't want to be their enemy.)
- have faith in their ability to find a solution. (They are not put off by other people saying they will never achieve it.)
- have confidence in their ability to stand the pace under pressure. (You would notice that they seem to have endless energy.)
- concentrate on the main issues and don't get side-tracked by unimportant details. (If a meeting wanders off the agenda, they would point out that it had done so.)
- can ignore their own inner demons which may be urging them to give in and give up. (If you saw signs of despondency in their face, voice or demeanour, you might also notice that sooner or later they would absent themselves for a moment, either physically or mentally. They would then return to the 'fray' with a new positive, calm demeanour.)

> Thrivers are as stubborn as oxen when they need to be!

Hopefully, you now have a clear idea of what I mean when I am referring to these qualities. As you were reading my descriptive lists, I wonder if you were able to recognize some of your own qualities and behaviours. I am sure many of you already have some of the Thriver personality package, but the big question is, of course, *do you have enough?*

If you are beginning to suspect that your Quality Kitbag is on the light side, don't worry. The good news is that all these qualities *can* be developed. The bad news is that if you don't take action soon, your task will probably become harder (though rarely impossible!). It is fundamental 'psychological law' that personal qualities, beliefs and behaviours are self-reinforcing.

- People who lack trust often find themselves automatically drawn to people who are likely to let them down, rarely notice opportunities for success and happiness, and regularly set themselves up for failure.
- People who lack humility don't notice their mistakes or blame others for them, and unconsciously seek out 'lesser mortals' for friends and colleagues.
- People who are inefficient often drift unknowingly into making such a mess of projects that they reach a point where they are indeed beyond the rescue of even the most obsessive organization.
- People who lack versatility can get stuck so deeply in a rut that change becomes more and more frightening and harder to survive.

So, having rung the warning bells to raise your anxiety levels, I'll now try to be helpful. (Perhaps I've seen too many TV cop shows where they use these push/pull tactics to induce co-operation!)

Here's an exercise which will help you choose where to begin your self-help programme.

Instant Exercise – How Full Is My Thriver Quality Kitbag?

- Re-read the list of Thriver qualities, but this time use my examples as a checklist for *yourself.*
- Then give yourself a score on a scale of 0–10 (0 indicating that this quality is non-existent in you, and 10 indicating

that you have more than your fair share of this quality!). You can enter these in the boxes below, but use pencil if you want to re-use this exercise for anyone else or would like to do it again in a few months' time to check on your progress.

CATHERINE COOKSON 1906–1998

Catherine was born illegitimate and endured a childhood of extreme poverty and hardship including being sexually assaulted by her mother's boyfriend. It was during these years that she began to write stories, but her interest and talent were never taken seriously. When she was 20 she submitted a play to a correspondence school and was 'strongly advised' not to take up writing as a career. Much of her adult life continued to be as unhappy as her childhood, and in 1944 she had a severe mental breakdown. As part of her unofficial therapy, she joined a writer's circle and started to produce her prolific output of best-selling novels. A further serious setback (writer's cramp) hit her in 1961, but again she persevered through it and dictated the rest of her books. In her later years she was given an honorary degree and made a Dame of the British Empire.

T *rusting*   ❑
H *umble*   ❑
R *esponsible*   ❑
I *ngenious*   ❑
V *ersatile*   ❑
E *fficient*   ❑
R *esolute*   ❑

During the next week, make a contract with yourself to try to develop one of the qualities which you have scored reasonably highly on, but would still like to improve. Use the 'Tips' in the following section to help guide you in that direction. After working for one or two weeks on your strongest qualities, you then can begin to look at your weaker areas.

Self-help Programme to Develop Thriver Qualities

> Life is not the way it's supposed to be. It's the way it is. The way you cope with it is what makes the difference.
>
> VIRGINIA SATIR

I have designed this section as a set of self-help exercises. Each section focuses on one of the qualities and is itself subdivided under four headings:

1 REFLECTION

2 TIPS

3 INSTANT WORKOUT

4 ACTION PLAN

Each section is marked by a different symbol to make it easy to identify.

Let me briefly explain what each is about.

REFLECTION

I suggest you start by first taking a little time to think generally about this quality and in particular *how* and *why* it may be problematic for you. To give you an idea of where and how to start, I will first share some of *my own personal reflections*.

Secondly, I will don my professional hat and give you a list of *common causes* of problems with this quality. These examples have been drawn from my experience of helping very many clients and the research I have read on this subject.

You may think this kind of reflection is an unnecessary step (and you might be right! – You could indeed be the kind of person who doesn't need to understand the cause of a problem before taking action to put it right). But many people I know are like me – they feel compelled to gain some measure of understanding of how their problem developed. If I don't *try* to obtain this before I start working on it, I find it difficult to motivate myself and accept that it is within my power to repair my own psychological damage.

If you are a newcomer to personal development work, I would recommend that you at least try the exercise. It certainly can't hurt you and you may find it interesting. It could also prove to be useful later because it will give you an insight into the difficulties other people can experience.

I then ask you to reflect on the specific areas in your everyday life which could benefit from some attention. This will help you to keep your self-help goals manageable. (I'm sure you don't want to give yourself unnecessary setbacks by overwhelming yourself with unrealistic action plans!)

TIPS

These are essentially a few suggestions. They are drawn from my own life experience and my experience of helping other people develop these qualities. Feel free to adapt them or add to them. You can also reject them, of course, but I hope that simply reading them will be a useful trigger. I know that when I want to change a habit, it helps me to look at an article or a book on the subject or even ask a friend for ideas. I may not take the 'advice', but at least in the process of obtaining it I have stimulated my own thinking brain and, as a result, have a better idea of what *I* need to do.

INSTANT WORKOUT

This is an exercise which I suggest you do immediately. It will help reinforce the learning from the rest of the section and stir your motivational juices!

ACTION PLAN

This is your goal-setting exercise. We now know through research that we are more likely to achieve our goals if we write them down. There is a space for you to do so in this book, but you may prefer to put them on a separate piece of paper or card and pin them up somewhere where you will bump into them from time to time.

We also know that it is useful to share our goals with another person, especially one who is willing to jog our memory in an *encouraging* way.

Becoming More Trusting

> In spite of everything I still believe that people are really good at heart.
>
> ANNE FRANK

REFLECTION

The roots of my own problem with trust go back to my formative toddler days. I was, like all children of alcoholics and unstable parents, continually let down. When my mother was in an 'up' phase my world was full of fun and warmth, but when she was 'down' that world collapsed. Looking through my child's eyes, these ups and downs must have been frightening because they would have appeared so totally inexplicable and unpredictable. Not surprisingly, I grew up *expecting* life to let me down again and again, and of course that's just what it did. I become an expert at making sure that life had no other choice! For example, I was an intelligent child, but did 'inexplicably' stupid things in exams, which ensured that I didn't achieve my full potential over and over again. (Attempting to answer questions on subjects which I had never studied was my particular speciality!)

In early adulthood, I drifted into unsuitable jobs in the most under-resourced social work organizations with the most chronically disturbed clients and burnt-out, cynical colleagues. In the meantime I was also dooming my personal life to fail me. I scorned all offers from the 'good guys' (I thought they were boring!) and fell into the arms of a succession of renowned rogues. So experience after experience 'proved' to me that in this world you could trust no one – not even yourself.

The story of the recovery of my trust in the world is a long one, but the essence of it is simple. I took control of my life and behaviour and made a *conscious* effort to try trusting myself and the world to ensure that I set myself up for success rather than failure.

For many years this was not easy to do. I felt I was being 'phony' because the 'real me' still felt 'naturally' pulled towards the losers and impossible challenges. I had continually to remind myself that there was nothing natural about being so untrusting of life (it's quite the opposite, as I hope you know!) and that no new behaviour feels genuine until it has become a habit.

Like most converts to a cause, I then began to over-use my new habit. I became too trusting. I had to burn my fingers several times before I learned to build in a *limited* degree of caution. Nowadays I still get the occasional scorched fingers, but the pain of these is infinitely more bearable than the hell-fire which my former cynicism and scepticism plunged me into whenever I met the slightest of setbacks.

Here are a few common reasons why some people are not as **trusting** as they need or want to be:

- being the victim of an overdose of unlucky experiences which they felt powerless to control (e.g. from late trains and robberies to world recessions and hurricanes)
- being repeatedly let down by people they love or need, especially at an early age
- making a series of mistakes which they have denied to themselves or covered up
- experiencing a series of mysterious failures (e.g. not being told why they didn't get the job, or why their partner no longer loves them)
- being born with an unreliable or 'quirky' body (making them more prone to sudden illness or accident)
- being surrounded by people who never change (and perhaps never want to change or believe you can either!).

Have any of these examples started ringing bells for you?

Has your ability to trust been damaged? If so, do you know how and when that happened?

Are there any areas in your life which would particularly benefit if you could be more trusting (e.g. with certain people or in certain situations)?

TIPS FOR BECOMING MORE TRUSTING

- Ask an acquaintance whom you know to be trusting if you can have a short chat with them. Explain what you are trying to do and that you just want to 'pick their brains'. Tell them that you want to understand what it is like to be someone who is trusting. Assuming that you don't set yourself up for failure by choosing someone who is very busy and preoccupied, you won't be rejected. Neither will you be considered stupid for making such an unusual request. I assure you that your chosen person will be flattered and only too willing to talk about a positive quality in themselves which they may never have fully appreciated. You will be encouraged and motivated and may even make a new friend.
- Vow to meet a wider circle of people. For example, make it a priority for the next six months to look *outside* your usual sources when recruiting friends, colleagues, staff or even soul-mates.
- When you note yourself thinking or speaking negatively about possible outcomes, visualize yourself putting on an imaginary pair of rose-coloured glasses and then use your mind's eye to *see* the opposite outcome actually happening. Allow yourself to sense in your body the pleasure which you would feel. Weird as this exercise might sound, *trust* me (try!) that it works. You would have implanted a possible positive scenario in the memory bank of your brain. The more of these you store up, the more trusting you will automatically begin to feel.

(Remember, when your brain does its filing, it does not make a distinction between imagined and real memories.)
- As a reminder, you could keep some real pink spectacles, or a picture of a pair, in a handy place.
- If you find this kind of imaginative exercise too 'difficult' to do, give yourself some regular practice in the art of creative visualization or take a class on the subject. There are tips on page 73 on how to do these effectively for yourself.
- Do some emotional healing work on one or more past hurts (see Further Reading).
- Remind yourself from time to time that your immediate goal is only to *behave* in a more trusting manner. (For example, you don't have to *believe* that only good can emerge from a setback – but acting as though this is the truth will increase your chances of finding a solution which could lead to a positive outcome.)

INSTANT WORKOUT FOR BECOMING MORE TRUSTING

- Sit in a relaxed but well-supported position and take three deep breaths.
- If you are reading this in a private place, close your eyes. In a calm, firm voice repeat out loud the following three affirmations approximately 10 times.

  1 *I can trust*
  2 *I trust both myself and others*
  3 *I enjoy being a trusting person*

- If you are not in a private place, you could repeat these affirmations in your mind and, to reinforce their power, write them down several times.
- Think of a specific positive outcome which could result from you being more trusting during the next couple of weeks.
- Now, with your eyes closed, use your imagination to visualize the scene and allow your body to sense the pleasure you would feel.

ACTION PLAN FOR BECOMING MORE TRUSTING

Over the next month my specific target area for increasing my trust will be:

_____

_____

(e.g. a particular relationship/set of people/situation/self)

In six months' time I will be able to:

_____

_____

I will reward myself by:

_____

_____

CHARLES DARWIN 1809–1882

Charles had his first serious setback when his beloved mother died when he was eight years old. He was reared by three sisters who constantly found fault with him. His father also 'predicted' that he would be a disgrace to his family. In spite of having innumerable setbacks from being a semi-invalid all his life, he proved his father to be spectacularly misguided. Charles became Britain's greatest biologist and produced the groundbreaking theory of evolution.

Becoming More Humble

REFLECTION

In view of the fact that much of my life's work has centred around helping people to build their confidence, it may seem strange that I should now be writing about the need to build humility. This is because, of course, humility has now developed many negative as well as positive connotations. But, it is its *virtues* which I am suggesting that you build. I have already listed some of these on page 4, but it may help to clarify my meaning a little further by sharing *my own working definition*, which is:

humility: to be conscious of your failings and the limits of your strengths and potential

Although many people might include words like servility, lowliness or self-abasement in their definitions, I would like to make it very clear that I am certainly *not* interested in building any quality which humiliates or abuses the weak, the powerless and the disadvantaged (*even* if it could make a success out of a setback!). On the contrary, I firmly believe that humility, in conjunction with the other qualities, can strengthen our inner and outer confidence. It does not need to be accompanied by demeaning, self-destructive victim-style thoughts or behaviour. In reality, of course it often is. So I would certainly understand if anyone reading this is feeling slightly sceptical or anxious about becoming more humble. If you are one of these people, please don't skip this section, just grant me a few more minutes to convince you!

Common reasons why people may think of being **humble** as negative:

- being witness to a humble loved one being physically or emotionally abused (e.g. many of my overly-arrogant clients witnessed a self-effacing parent being hurt by aggressive behaviour from the other parent)
- being humiliated as a child and then growing up thinking that humility attracts humiliation (no, it doesn't have to!)

- having an unhappy experience of being in a servile position and having an association in your mind between servility and humility (another misunderstanding!)
- being part of a group which is or has been discriminated against and believing that humility always encourages discrimination and threatens human rights' struggles (yet another! – think of just two powerful, well-respected humble figures of our present age – Archbishop Tutu and Mother Teresa)
- having images planted in their mind which make associations between humility and a seemingly unattractive lifestyle (e.g. my own example was that I spent much of my childhood in the presence of nuns who were constantly revered for their humility, but very many of them did not appear to be enjoying their impoverished, secluded life)
- overdosing on the wrong kind of self-esteem building or assertiveness training (i.e. the kind which does not take into account the value of compromise and the importance of respecting the rights and feelings of others)
- holding an erroneous belief that needing and requesting help from someone more expert than yourself is a sign of weakness (another of my own deeply-rooted problem areas. It was developed because as a child it seemed to me that the most respected people in my warped world were the ones who didn't need help – '*Look at him, he just gets on with it*')
- hearing too often sayings which make associations between humility and punishment or humiliation (e.g. 'You'll be eating humble pie if you're not careful' and 'Humble hearts have humble desires')
- worshipping martyr saints who were especially renowned for their humility, and mistakenly assuming that it was their humility that led to their premature violent death (when it was, in reality, other people's arrogance that killed them)
- believing that humility and poverty are inextricably linked (the reality is that arrogance is the cause of *many* an economic downfall)

- being over-adored and over-indulged as a child (and growing up thinking superiority is the way to gain and retain affection).

Can you relate to any of these reasons?

Can you think of any other reasons why you are not as humble as you would like to be?

If so, are you aware of any *specific* areas where you find it difficult to be humble?

> To finally recognize our own invisibility is to finally be on the path toward visibility.
>
> MITSUYE YAMADA

TIPS FOR BECOMING MORE HUMBLE

- Take a course in an area which interests you but for which you have not developed any special skill (my Argentine Tango lessons are currently a very good antidote to any grandiosity which might have seeped into my personality).
- Read some autobiographies of successful people outside your area of expertise (better still, try to meet one of these in person).
- Visit regularly the world's man-made wonders (you may not need to take to the air to see the Taj Mahal; there is probably something to see locally which will do the job just as well. In my current hometown of Portsmouth there are some pretty stunning ships to ogle admiringly. In my previous hometown, there was a famous cathedral).
- Go to a museum or historical exhibition (a recent visit to one on the history of Chinese civilization in the new Guggenheim Museum in Bilbao, Spain, gave me a dose of humility which will last me several years. A less recent visit to the Anne Frank museum in Amsterdam did the same).
- Take a walk up (or around, if you are me!) a mountain and gaze at the stars. If you can't do that, go to a Planetarium or watch a TV programme/video on astronomy.

- Ask for help from at least three different people every week for a month.

INSTANT WORKOUT FOR BECOMING MORE HUMBLE

Make a list of 10 serious mistakes you have made in your life.

List three memorable occasions when you were very grateful for receiving help from someone else.

> Do not fear mistakes. There are none - it just depends on what you make of the next note.
>
> MILES DAVIS

Name 10 subjects about which you could *never* write a book (but would not mind reading about if written by someone else).

ACTION PLAN FOR BECOMING MORE HUMBLE

Over the next month my specific target area for increasing my humility will be:

_____

_____

By the end of six months I will have:

_____

_____

I will reward myself by:

_____

_____

> Surviving is important but thriving is elegant.
>
> MAYA ANGELOU

Please note: don't overdo this part of your programme. Thrivers need self-esteem as well!

MAYA ANGELOU 1928–

Maya was born in the southern US, well before the Civil Rights Movement came into being. She survived a traumatic childhood, being raped at eight and becoming mute for five years, a victim of racism, and then an unmarried mother at 16. Among her many achievements against formidable odds she became San Francisco's first black bus conductor; the first black female Hollywood director; a highly successful actress; best-selling novelist, poet and professor. She wrote and delivered the presidential inauguration poem for President Clinton. Through her autobiographical account of her childhood, poetry and media appearances, she drew the world's attention to the trauma and pain of sexual abuse in an unforgettable way. Through her media work, she has used her celebrity status to encourage millions of women from disadvantaged backgrounds to make more of their lives.

Becoming More Responsible

REFLECTION

> The ultimate measure of a man is not where he stands in moments of comfort and convenience, but where he stands at times of challenge and controversy.
>
> MARTIN LUTHER KING

Looking back over my own experience of coping with setbacks, I know that I would put my sense of responsibility very high on the list of qualities which have helped me thrive. But in my younger days I can recall the word 'responsible' used to induce feelings of panic in me. In those days I cannot recall having a clear vision of what kind of life I wanted for myself, but I am quite certain it would not have included writing this chapter! I know that I associated this quality with being tied down to an inhibiting lifestyle, staid, stale relationships – and being old!

My feelings of panic were partly induced by the normal rebelliousness of youth, but they also had their roots in my early childhood. My family circumstances were such that, in order to survive I had to become too responsible too quickly. In an unconscious search for psychological equilibrium, I felt compelled to put freedom and 'living for the moment' as my primary goals for many years.

I have since found that many of my clients have had similar histories, but equally many have had just the opposite! So let's look at some of the many reasons why people develop problems in this area, and you can check whether any of these have any significance for you:

- having to look after a parent who was sick or emotionally unstable when they were a child
- having to look after a sibling before they were themselves mature enough to do so
- being *overly* encouraged into sensible and disciplined habits in order to achieve a goal such as high grades at school or music or sporting accolades (particularly when your peers were out having enviable fun)
- loving and admiring gifted or beautiful role-models who were irresponsible (e.g. a 'colourful' wayward father or anarchic pop icons)
- being emotionally or physically hurt by parents who were irresponsible
- having low self-esteem and (especially while still at an impressionable age) joining a 'gang' with a rebellious culture
- being too dependent for friendship on a religion or cult which gives duty a *much* higher priority than personal fulfilment and happiness

- having a lack of fun in life (which can give rise to the temptation of doing things too often 'just for the hell of it')
- getting married 'too young'
- living or working with people who make 'heavy weather' of being too responsible
- not being rewarded enough for being responsible (e.g. being taken for granted at work, especially if less responsible, colourful colleagues are attracting attention or 'getting away with murder').

Did you relate to any of these reasons?

Is there any other reason why you might not always be as responsible as you would like to be?

Is there any area in your life which might particularly benefit if you were to become more responsible?

TIPS FOR BECOMING MORE RESPONSIBLE

- Read an autobiography of someone you admire who has led a responsible life (this could be even more effective if the person had a history of irresponsibility and then saw the light!).
- Make a note of what you would stand to gain by becoming more responsible (e.g. 'I would have fewer financial crises!' or 'I would become a better role-model for my children').
- Make a note of what you may stand to lose if you do not become more responsible (e.g. 'My relationship with ...' or 'My chance of gaining promotion').
- Make a list of 'warning signals' which would indicate that you are not being as responsible as you would like to be (e.g. 'Going to bed later than 11 p.m. on a week-day' or 'Spending more than ... per month').
- Ask someone to tell you if you start using 'victim' language (e.g. 'Why me, again?' or 'This is just typical of my luck').

- Ask someone to tell you when you start blaming someone or something for your feelings instead of taking full responsibility for them (e.g. you say 'He makes me angry' instead of 'I become angry when he .... so I will have to ....' or 'This weather always depresses me' instead of 'It's raining again today, so if I don't want to get depressed, I'll have to ....'

- Use the Emotional Healing Strategy when you have been let down or hurt (see page 132).

- When someone misunderstands you, and you start to feel irritated by their 'stupidity' or 'lack of concentration', ask them how you could have improved your message or style of communicating.

- Set aside some regular times in your schedule when you can indulge your need or wish to be a little irresponsible with time. (I know that I am much more prepared to settle down to unappealing duties and timetables if I know I can look forward to a holiday without my watch.)

- Allow yourself regular extravagances. Calculate the quantity of these in the light of your budget and principles without reference to what anyone else may think. (Don't forget that the more restrictive your budget is and the heavier your financial responsibilities, the more you need to programme in the occasional extravagance and treat. If you don't, you'll find yourself resenting your responsibility and there is a danger you will eventually start self-sabotaging unconsciously.)

INSTANT WORKOUT FOR BECOMING MORE RESPONSIBLE

Replace the following five sentences starting with 'If only ...' with responsible language. (These are examples of victim language. The phrase 'if only' is a clue to its presence and can be used as a very useful warning signal. Sometimes these two words may not be actually spoken, but if you could insert them without losing the meaning of what you are saying, you can be pretty certain that you are operating in a non-responsible mode. Doing this exercise will give you some practice at re-phrasing.)

Examples:

'If only he had listened to me, we wouldn't have been in this mess.'

'Obviously, we are not communicating well. I'll have to think of a way of getting the message across to him more effectively.'

'If only I were rich, this wouldn't have been a problem.'

'This little setback is certainly going to cost more to put right than I can comfortably afford. I'll have to spend some time looking at how I can get hold of some more money.'

1   'If only I'd come in 10 minutes earlier, I'd have caught him.'

_____

_____

2   'If only it hadn't rained.'

_____

_____

3   'If only there were more jobs around, it would be so much easier.'

_____

_____

4   'If only we had more staff, she wouldn't have complained.'

_____

_____

5   'If only my mother had really cared about me.'

_____

_____

ACTION PLAN FOR BECOMING MORE RESPONSIBLE

Over the next month I will increase my ability to be responsible by:

_____

_____

In six months' time I will be able to:

_____

_____

I will reward myself by:

_____

_____

FRANK McCOURT 1931–

Survived a childhood of extreme poverty and hardship in Limerick which he put behind him in order to thrive as a teacher in the US. When he retired, he wrote a best-selling masterpiece about his life as a child that is renowned for making people roar with laughter as well as cry with compassion. He said of his childhood: 'I wonder how I managed to survive it at all. It was of course, a miserable childhood: the happy childhood is hardly worth your while.'

Becoming More Ingenious

REFLECTION

> In the middle of difficulty lies opportunity.
>
> ALBERT EINSTEIN

Ingenuity is a quality that is produced by the creative centres in our mind. It must be one of the most important, if not the most important, qualities for dealing with setbacks. It enables us to come up with *new* solutions to seemingly impossible problems.

Our constantly changing and challenging world demands more and more ingenuity from all of us. But the good news is that we (unlike previous generations) now know how this quality can be developed in almost anyone who decides they need or want more of it.

It may be true that some people are more blessed with genes which make this kind of thinking relatively easy, but research is indicating that most humans are only currently using a tiny percentage of every aspect of their brain's potential. So even if you are not destined to make history with an incredible invention or great creative work, you could, in theory, be much more ingenious than you are at present.

So let's look at why you (and probably most people you know) may not have developed as much of this quality as you would have liked.

Common reasons why people may not be as ingenious as they could be:

- Their parents or siblings may have, consciously or unconsciously, 'put down' or punished their early experiments with ingenuity (e.g. laughing at ideas from imaginary friends/becoming cross at attempts to decorate a boring wall with lipstick).
- Their parents may have had a psychological need to have things done according to their 'proven' way or the traditional way, and may not have been able to tolerate the anxiety which accompanies the risk of an experimental approach.

- Their creative thinking powers may not have been given adequate scope for development at school (the curriculum being heavily weighted to learning by rote or using a more logical approach to problem-solving).
- They may have led an overly sheltered and protected life as a child, and rarely been presented with opportunities to come up with solutions to new challenges.
- Their own attempts to be ingenious may have been regularly outshone by a parent's or sibling's greater creative or imaginary powers.
- Their adult life in general may have been stuck in one rut for too long so their creative thinking 'muscles' have weakened.
- They may live in a repressive society which insists on everyone toeing the 'party' line and severely punishing individual ingenuity.
- They may practise a religion which lays down too many dictates about the right and wrong way to live life, in order to guarantee a tolerable place in eternity.
- They may have low self-esteem. Inventors and pioneers very often have to endure extended periods of ridicule before their novel ideas are accepted. For example, the inventor of the umbrella had to walk around Hyde Park in London with his ingenious prototype being laughed at for two years before he was taken seriously. Living in rainy Britain, I owe a debt of gratitude to this man's robust self-esteem!

Have you experienced, or are you, experiencing, any of the above?

Can you think of any other reason why you may not be as ingenious as you would like to be?

Is there any particular area in your life which would particularly benefit if you were to become more ingenious?

TIPS FOR BECOMING MORE INGENIOUS

- Visit exhibitions and museums of inventions at least twice a year.
- The moment you find yourself feeling bored by doing a routine chore, ask yourself 'If I *had* to do this task another way, what would be my options?'
- Once a week, try changing one ingredient in the recipe which you are using (without looking at another cookery book or ringing Mum!).
- Seize every opportunity to play games which stretch your imagination such as Charades or Pictionary. (Don't wait for Christmas!)
- While you are standing in queues, imagine what entertainment you would (if you could!) arrange to have to amuse everyone.
- If you are bored on a train, coach or plane journey, close your eyes and imagine that you are being taken to somewhere other than your destination.
- Collect inspirational articles (or newspaper obituaries) about inventors or other ingenious thinkers, especially those who have found new ways to thrive on setbacks. Keep them in an attractive file and put it on the coffee table so you can browse through and show them to friends. (Ask them to add to your file.)
- Read (and take heed of!) Chapter 3 on mind fitness, paying special attention to the section on creativity.
- Keep your self-esteem well boosted and test its strength from time to time by trying out some 'wacky' ideas which you know might raise a laugh or snigger.

INSTANT WORKOUT FOR BECOMING MORE INGENIOUS

Answer the following five questions:

1   If you wanted to meet new friends, what could you do differently this weekend to make sure this happened?

2 If you could redecorate the room you are in now with three different colours, what would they be?

3 If you decided not to go on holiday next year, name three different ways you could spend the money you would save.

4 If you had been given a very substantial grant to develop a new product for cleaning your house/office or maintaining your garden, what new appliance would you like to see invented?

5 If you wanted to plan a surprise 'happening' for your colleagues at work (or another set of friends in another organization) what would you do?

> It takes a lot of time to be a genius, you have to sit around so much doing nothing, really doing nothing.
>
> GERTRUDE STEIN

ACTION PLAN FOR BECOMING MORE INGENIOUS

Over the next month I will increase my ingenuity by:

_____

_____

In six months' time I will be able to:

_____

_____

I will reward myself by:

_____

_____

FFYONA CAMPBELL

Ffyona, who was born in England, completed an 11-year 20,000 mile walk around the world, starting with £50 in her pocket. Before leaving home at 16, she had moved house 24 times and was educated at 15 different schools. She endured incredible hardships on her journey, but also found a way of overcoming many blocks to success within herself. She publicly shared her past history of selfishness, cheating and heroin addiction in an inspiring book.

Becoming More Versatile

REFLECTION

Versatility is making a comeback. For most of my lifetime, this personal quality has been out of fashion. As I grew up, the message my contemporaries and I received was that there was little future left for the 'Jacks of all trades'. We were therefore forced to specialize prematurely at school, and then when we hit the world of work we were urged to 'niche-market' our skills and talents.

For some people this was undoubtedly good advice, but I can remember very clearly feeling resentful at having to narrow my options so early and so rigidly. I wanted to study and do everything – even the old-fashioned options that no one else wanted to do like classical Greek and embroidery! My choices weren't made any easier by the fact that I seemed to be more or less equally competent at a wide range of subjects and activities. Instead of valuing my versatility, I longed to be undeniably brilliant and mesmerized by one 'true calling' in my life. How I envied the 'geniuses' who seemed so totally absorbed and fulfilled as they perfected their one particular art, sport, craft or scientific skill. As a good 'all-rounder' I felt that I was doomed to be uninspired and unrenowned.

When my younger daughter, Laura, hit the same frustrations at a critical time in her life, I knew just how she felt. But at least by then I was in a position to reassure her that:

- she wasn't a freak (she was like me!). She could choose to be proud of her multifaceted nature.
- she would eventually find that there were many advantages to being so versatile. I gave her examples of how my own versatility had helped me weather a whole range of unforeseen ups and downs in both my personal and professional life. When required I had found it relatively easy to adapt to the different lifestyles my changing fortunes brought, and also to learn new 'tricks' for my trade when the world of work forced me to diversify. I knew from my experience as a therapist that many other people did not find this kind of flexibility so easy to find within themselves. They were either not so naturally blessed with the genes of versatility, or they had had it strangled by one or more of the following kinds of experiences in their life.

Common reasons why some people are not as **versatile** as they could be.

They may have:

- had parents who encouraged and rewarded a limited range of activities and studies
- been brought up in a society which had strict gender stereotyping
- had a lack of opportunity – we know, for example, that many children have been unable to develop innate additional musical, craft, cooking, computer and communication skills simply because their schools or communities lacked the facilities or teachers to help them
- been in a family (or other group) where every member is a specialist in certain roles and tasks. Although it obviously makes some sense for a group to 'play' on the strengths of its individuals, this can lead to a loss of confidence in other areas of competence. Our own family did this unknowingly. It wasn't until my daughter Laura died that I realized what had happened. She had become our 'artistic director' – we had all drifted into becoming

dependent on her for making all our decisions which involved a choice of style and colour. Unfortunately it took the loss of Laura to make us aware that we were capable of doing this very adequately (but perhaps not perfectly!) for ourselves

- been too much of a perfectionist and not allowed themselves to do tasks which they may only be able to do adequately but not excellently. (Since reaching a standard of living which has allowed me to employ a professional decorator, the impossible standards I now set for my own attempts now make a job I used to enjoy too stressful to attempt!)

- become lazy! – only bothering to practise the skills which come easily. (I used to be perfectly capable of adding together a column of figures, but since drifting into dependency on the calculators in my computer and my husband's brain, I have lost this simple skill.)

Do any of these examples remind you of similar blocks to the development of your own versatility?

Can you think of any other reason why you may not be as versatile as you would like to be?

Would an increase in your versatility be helpful to you in any specific area of your life?

TIPS FOR BECOMING MORE VERSATILE

- Make a habit of doing some temporary role-reversals with your family or colleagues. (If you've seen the film *Trading Places*, you'll know what I mean!) Stepping into each other's shoes for a while will also improve your understanding of each other and help you to communicate better. It was a 'game' my children loved playing and I found that it strengthened my humility as well as my versatility!

- Don't forget that if you are 'playing' it seriously you will have to do it long enough to enable everyone to work through the first embarrassing and awkward stages. Many successful organizations have benefited from this kind of exercise and now insist that key management staff exchange roles from time to time and do secondments in complementary but contrasting businesses. But what's good for the goose should also be good for the gander, so why don't we all do it?

- Take your holidays in areas which have very different customs and rituals from the ones you are used to, and then 'when in Rome *do* as the Romans do.' For example, if you go to Wales, go to a rugby match or local pub and sing-a-along; drink your coffee out of a bowl in France; shake hands with everybody you meet in Denmark; bow if you are in Japan; dance the Sevillanas if you find yourself amidst a Spanish Fiesta (that's one for my New Year's resolution list).

- Eat more frequently in foreign or different styles of restaurants (and don't forget to eat your curry with a chapati; your noodles with chopsticks; your spaghetti without a knife; your sushi sitting on the floor, and your fish and chips with your fingers!).

- Join a drama group or class and act a variety of roles (especially the ones which are very different from your own character).

- Join an assertiveness training class (who doesn't need more of that good thing!) and volunteer to do as much role-playing as you can.

- Offer to help at a toddlers' playgroup or holiday play scheme, or just join in children's fantasy games. Children have no hang-ups about versatility and will encourage you to drop your inhibitions. (Do you remember when you too thought you could do everything?!)

- For half an hour a week, practise using your non-dominant hand and leg for doing whatever task you happen to be doing. For example: paying for your newspaper with coins; buttering bread; washing in the shower; kicking a ball for the dog or the children; watering the garden – but not driving the car, please. (Ambidextrous readers please pass on this one.)

> When I ask survivors if there is any quality or trait that contributes most to being a survivor, they usually answer without hesitation. They say either 'flexibility' or 'adaptability'.
>
> DR AL SIEBERT - RESEARCH PSYCHOLOGIST SPECIALIZING IN SURVIVOR SKILLS

INSTANT WORKOUT FOR BECOMING MORE VERSATILE

- Name at least three skills which you used to have and have allowed to turn rusty. Decide which of these could be most useful for you today and include its development in your action plan. (You may need to go back to examine the talents you began to develop at school or in early adulthood.) Many of my clients have also dramatically improved the quality of their lives by doing this exercise. Some, for example, have started up new hobbies such as acting or singing while others have taken a new career turn by rekindling their aptitude for language learning, writing or teaching.
- Name three activities which you have always wanted to try but never given yourself the time or resources to have a go at. Add at least one of these to your list of resolutions for next year (or next month!).
- Write out the list of Thriver qualities 10 times with your non-dominant hand. (Use your toes if you find this hand exercise too easy!)

ACTION PLAN FOR BECOMING MORE VERSATILE

Over the next month I will increase my versatility by:

_____

_____

In six months' time I will be able to:

_____

_____

I will reward myself by:

_____

_____

MARIE CURIE 1867–1936

Against the formidable odds of the male-dominated world of science in the 19th century, the Polish-born Marie Curie made a highly successful career. At a breakthrough point in her research, she received a bitter blow. Her husband, who was also a renowned scientist and her research partner, was killed in an accident. She continued their research on her own and in spite of many defeats and humiliations at the hands of the Academy of Science, as well as the press and society, she went on to make her groundbreaking discoveries about radium. She also became the first woman to teach at the Sorbonne and received a Nobel prize.

Becoming More Efficient

REFLECTION

> There can be no happiness if the things we believe in are different from the things we do.
>
> FREYA STARK

I remember a friend recently said to me 'You're incredibly efficient, aren't you? No wonder you can achieve so much.' I was quite taken aback, because I have *never* considered myself to be as efficient as I would like to be.

Afterwards, I admit I indulged in a bit of self-congratulation. After all, I have had to surmount many a steep learning curve to reach my current level of efficiency. By inclination I am what is popularly called 'an ideas person'. I often fantasize about how much easier and more productive my life would be if it were being *totally* organized by a highly efficient team of support staff. I would sit and contemplate my navel until the bright ideas began to flow and then hand over the seedlings of my project to the team who would put it into much more highly skilled and well-managed practice than I could ever hope to do.

But unfortunately that is likely to remain fantasy for ever. The reality is that I have been forced (poor me!) to find good-enough 'slaves' within myself!

It is some comfort to know that this reliance on my own inner administrative self has actually helped me to become a Thriver. Commonly, when we come across a setback, we have to be self-reliant anyway. The nature of many life crises means that the structure of our everyday lives, roles and relationships are disrupted. Our normal routines may be suddenly turned upside-down, our resources strained and the people who usually support us may themselves be struggling to 'hold their own'. This means that often in our most difficult times, we are unable to count so easily on others. The irony is that these are the times when we need the routine management of our lives to be working even more efficiently than before.

I first learned this lesson early in my adult life when my life limped continuously from setback to setback (most of my own making, I must admit!). Organization of my day-to-day affairs became increasingly chaotic, and the problems that this in itself presented undoubtedly accelerated my descent down the spiral of despair. There was little hope of solving my major problems because any remnant of motivation and energy was used to 'fire-fight' the mountains of mini problems caused by missed deadlines, unpaid bills and forgotten appointments (not to mention shortages of clean knickers and edible food!).

Now I find that the majority of people who come to me for help are in similar states. Before we can begin to address the major issues posed by the setback, they have to take steps to bring back some order into their everyday lives. Only then do they have adequate energy and concentration to confront questions such as 'Should I change career?', 'Should I move?' or 'Should I remarry?'

So why is being efficient so hard for some of us? Here are some common reasons:

- having over-indulgent parents who were over-solicitous of our everyday needs. Children usually need to suffer from chaos (especially of their own making) before they can appreciate the value of being efficient.
- being rewarded too easily for achievement as a child, and never having had the opportunity to learn the joys (?!) of delayed gratification. Gifted children who 'sailed through' school often do not know how to organize themselves when they later meet the more competitive and less immediately rewarding world of work.
- being 'suffocated' under the weight of excess discipline and organization imposed by others. This often leads to a rebellious attitude towards any form of organization.
- not having clear goals and priorities. Dithering about what should be done next is a common cause of inefficiency.
- lack of clear values. Dithering about whether something ought or ought not be done is increasingly common as people are now finding themselves lost in the moral maze that is characterizing our age. It is much easier to be efficient if we can operate within the guidelines of black-and-white principles. (I know that I'll always be tempted to put off making those awkward decisions which involve me spending time and energy immersing myself in the grey areas.)
- mistakenly believing that creative genius and efficiency can never be companions. (It is true that the birth of a creative idea emerges most easily when we take the reins off our logical thinking powers. But it is also true that we can do this much more readily and often if we can depend

on the security of efficient foundations to support and maintain us through periods of creative chaos.)

- trying to do too much in too little time
- trying to do too much with too few resources
- arrogance – believing that efficiency belongs in the realm of people whom we consider 'lesser mortals' because they are further down the social hierarchy (such as administrative staff, housekeepers, caretakers, garage mechanics or book-keepers). This is obviously a very hard reason to accept and one that is rarely openly acknowledged. It is however deeply embedded in most cultures and is more common than most of us would like to believe
- being indoctrinated with the myth that the only way to get a job done *properly* is to do it yourself, and therefore being reluctant to ask for help even when it would obviously aid efficiency to do so
- hedonism – being too reluctant to stop indulging in the pursuit of pleasure in favour of doing what appears to be boring, dull chores.

Can you understand some of the causes of your own lack of efficiency?

What areas of your life in particular could do with an organization overhaul?

TIPS FOR BECOMING MORE EFFICIENT

- Do regular time-management reviews (even if you have spent a fortune on several time-management courses which should have reformed you!). It helps to take stock of your progress and change your techniques and systems from time to time.
- Borrow or buy a new book or treat yourself to a new time-management diary or computer-based organizer programme. Try anything until you find something that works for you. My husband's solution cost him several

hundred pounds, but he wouldn't be without his giant tailor-made organizer. I have found that reminders and lists on different coloured post-it notes and a kitchen timer work best for me.

- If you have sunk into an 'inefficiency slump' and are looking and feeling dreary, give yourself an image 'makeover'. Change your clothing or hairstyle so that what you see in the mirror looks like a person who is organized and in control. Then smile at the new you! This exercise is not as silly as it sounds. It works because it is an affirmation in action. The image is sending a powerful symbolic message to your brain which is saying 'I am efficient and I like myself being efficient.' You will begin to feel more motivated. It can be a mistake to 'dress down' too sloppily for our less interesting tasks.

- Buy or make some colourful, decorated cards or post-it notes for your *daily prioritized* to-do lists.

- Plan an appropriate treat for each successfully completed to-do list, and add it to the bottom of your list. This way, the more challenging lists have their *just* rewards, and your self-esteem as well as your efficiency has a boost. (Yes, this *can* take place daily!)

- Before you make your list add an encouraging quote, saying or proverb at the top. The task of writing the quote out will help fix it in your mind and help motivate you through the day. Use some of the ones in this book or one from an appropriate collection. There are now many books packed full of pithy sayings to give us a boost during different kinds of difficult times.

- To avoid becoming bored with your regular chores or your mind wandering on to your problems, build some fun, interest or excitement into them. For example put on music or an audio-book while you are sorting, filing or ironing; build in a fun warm-up or team competition into routine meetings, or experiment with a 'Ministry of Silly Walks' method of getting from A to B. (This latter one is not recommended for the office, but could make vacuum cleaning or tidying up at home more challenging!)

- Burn appropriate aromatherapy oils when you know you may sink into a negative mood while doing certain tasks. For example, burn a calming essence (e.g. lavender or camomile) when you know that you have calls to make which could make you irritable or anxious. Burn an uplifting one (e.g. geranium or lemon) to invigorate you when you think you may become bored. If you are in an office situation, soak a handkerchief with the essence and give it a discreet sniff from time to time!
- Vary the timetables of your administrative tasks whenever you can, so they do not seem so repetitive.
- Ask an efficient friend or colleague for advice and, if they are willing, ask them to give you some feedback when they see you self-sabotaging with your old habits.
- Alternate uninspiring 'chores' with rewarding periods of work so that they do not have time to depress your mood. When we are in the midst of a setback, we are often more vulnerable to becoming depressed and disheartened. (*Ideally*, each of us should experiment for ourselves until we get the balance which produces our most efficient way of operating. So managers and parents beware! There is no golden rule to setting general schedules.)
- Give yourself (and your inner rebellious child?) some regular breaks from efficiency. For example, days at home or on holiday without a watch; one week a year without housework, or one morning a week when you don't do any administrative chores.
- Read Chapter 8.

INSTANT WORKOUT FOR BECOMING MORE EFFICIENT

Draw two pie-charts, similar to these examples, to illustrate how you are currently apportioning your time.

My Average Working Day

My Average Week-end Day

ACTION PLAN FOR BECOMING MORE EFFICIENT

Over the next month I will increase my efficiency by:

_____

_____

In six months' time I will be able to:

_____

_____

I will reward myself by:

_____

_____

LUDWIG VAN BEETHOVEN 1770–1827

Endured a childhood with a father who was continually violent, drunk and irresponsible. He managed to become one of the world's very greatest composers in spite of becoming progressively deaf. He expressed his feelings of despair and loneliness through his unique and passionate music, but most of his greatest works end in triumph and continue to inspire and uplift listeners all over the world.

Becoming More Resolute

REFLECTION

This is probably the most important quality of all for dealing with setbacks, and it

> I have discovered the secret that after climbing a great hill, one only finds that there are many more hills to climb.
>
> NELSON MANDELA

may well be the hardest to develop. The irony is that we would be able to acquire more of it much more easily if we had a good deal of it in the first place! After all, every difficult personal development challenge requires a strong resolve to help us persist and see us through the inevitable odd backslide into old habits.

As a child, I had a strong will and this undoubtedly helped me to survive better than most of my peers in the children's homes. It emerged mainly in the form of stubborn craftiness. If I wanted something, I might appear to take 'No' for an answer (I had no choice) but I wouldn't give up. I'd be determined to find a way around the problem, usually by means of a combination of charm and deceit.

Sadly, by the time I had reached my mid-twenties, this gift had been totally dissipated. Not only had I by then lost the will to persist through setbacks, I'd lost the will to live. It was a long hard job reclaiming and reinforcing my resolve, and even now I cannot afford to take it for granted. If I allow myself to become too tired or too stressed, it will ebb. Fortunately, I now know how to catch it before it gets to a dangerously low level. Many of the tips which I give in the later section are the ones I use to re-energize my own resolve.

How strong is your own resolve? Has yours too taken a battering on its journey to the present day? Can you identify with any of these common causes of weakened resolve?

- being continually set impossible challenges by parents or teachers, and growing up to believe that you will always fail
- seeing beloved role-models become unhappy or ill as a result of being too persistent with impossible challenges (e.g. a mother's unshakeable commitment to reforming a husband who did not want to change, or a father's relentless struggle to almost single-handedly right the wrongs and injustices of the giant organization which employed him)
- not being rewarded for overcoming a series of difficulties or allowed to take pride in yourself for doing so (e.g.

'Don't brag' and 'That's no more than I'd expect from you' attitudes)

- being given over-generalized and hurtful put-downs (as opposed to gentle teasing) about our resolve. One of my clients has never forgotten this remark she overheard a teacher make about her: 'She's a little madam, when she wants something there's no stopping her – I bet she'd do anything to get her own way.' I am sure that it is not a coincidence that she grew up to be someone who continually abandoned her own attempts to get her needs met the moment she felt (often wrongly) that she would hurt someone else's feelings

- being brought up in a family or society which has an overly high regard for short-term thinking and quick results

- not being rewarded or complimented for effort as well as achievement.

Do you think that you have become less resolute than you were at birth? (All babies appear to be very determined to me.)

Do you think that your development of this important quality has been hampered by your experiences or your current lifestyle?

Are there any areas in your life which would particularly benefit if you were more resolute?

> To be defeated and yet not surrender, that is victory.
>
> JOZEF PILSDULSKI - POLISH FREEDOM FIGHTER

TIPS FOR BECOMING MORE RESOLUTE

- Take time out to visualize the possible negative and positive outcomes of an action, giving more time and energy to the latter. For example:
  - if you are motivated by a wish not to disappoint a loved one, bring to your mind's eye a picture of their sad face;

if you don't want to repeat the same mistake, picture yourself making that mistake again

- if you want to be able to buy a certain kind of house, run a mental movie in your mind of yourself living in it for a weekend
- if you are aiming at gaining a certain job, run a mental movie of you doing some of its key tasks in front of an admiring audience.

- Set step-by-step goals – after a setback these need to be spaced even more closely together (see pages 169-172 for useful guidelines on goal-setting).

- Reward your good efforts as well as achievements. Remember that after a setback we often don't function at our best. It is hard to stop *feeling* inept and silly even though we may know in our mind that we are not actually going backwards. We therefore need more rewards than usual, and they need to be more nurturing than during times when we are feeling robust (e.g. an aromatherapy massage or delicious nutritional snack, rather than a new pair of socks or a glass of 'plonk').

- Ask friends to cheer you on. Tell them that you need an extra supply of compliments for a while. (Yes, that is allowed, even though you are building self-determination into your resolve. They would not be controlling *your* 'carrot', merely admiring your progress towards it.)

- Use assertiveness techniques to protect your energy and stop yourself getting side-tracked by other people (see pages 156-164 and Further Reading section).

- Use emotional management strategies to keep control of any counter-productive feelings and moods (see page 151 and Further Reading section).

> Great works are performed not by strength but by perseverance.
> SAMUEL JOHNSON

INSTANT WORKOUT FOR BECOMING MORE RESOLUTE

- Think of one occasion in your life when, through being determined and persistent, you *did* achieve success.
- Recall the scene in your mind's eye, and select one object that you see which could serve as a symbolic reminder of the occasion.
- Do a simple line drawing of that object (artistic talent not needed, and as long as this is not a borrowed book, you can draw on it now!). Practise repeating your drawing several times so that you can do it quickly and easily whenever and wherever you want to. You could later draw it on a number of post-it notes and use them as reminders on the fridge door, the loo seat, dressing table mirror, the car dashboard, the computer or the phone. Enlarge the drawing and the quantity of reminder post-it notes when you need to be particularly resolute.

ACTION PLAN FOR BECOMING MORE RESOLUTE

Over the next month I will increase my ability to stay resolute by:

_____

_____

In six months' time I will be able to:

_____

_____

I will reward myself by:

_____

_____

Always bear in mind that your own resolution to succeed is more important than any one thing.

ABRAHAM LINCOLN

NELSON MANDELA 1918–

Nelson was born in South Africa. His father died suddenly when he was nine years old and his life changed almost overnight. He was taken from his idyllic simple country life to live in the royal residence of the man who was to be his guardian for the next 10 years. When he became a freedom fighter (inside and outside gaol) against the apartheid regime, his life became famously full of setbacks that few other human beings would have survived. He also experienced many other setbacks in his personal life, including the loss of many close friends, the accidental death of his beloved son, and divorce. He won the Nobel Peace Prize and became one of the 20th century's greatest and most respected political leaders when he was elected as the first president of the new democratic South African Republic.

CHAPTER 2

Wheel 1:
The Personal
Skills that Propel
the Thriver

So let's imagine that you are now approximately six months down your personal development road. Like the cyclist on a journey of discovery, you have worked dutifully and successfully on developing

> Instead of seeing the rug being pulled from under us, we can learn to dance on a shifting carpet.
>
> THOMAS CRUM

your Quality Kitbag – your Thriver personality package. Your bag is at bursting point and now, quite understandably, you feel like sitting smugly back with a glass of champagne to await the next setback. Yes, you actually *want* a setback (well, a little one anyway!). Like the superbly trained boxer who can't wait to enter the ring, you too are keen to test your mettle against a real-life challenge.

But unfortunately, the champagne must wait. There's still some work to do. Thrivers with overflowing kitbags also need another essential tool – an extra sturdy, well-maintained bike!

So by all means pour yourself a small glass of wine and take a short rewarding break. But don't leave it too long before checking that your wheels can give you maximum support and propelling power.

In this chapter we are going to look at Wheel One – our Personal Skills Wheel. You will remember from the Introduction that this Wheel is made up of these three main sections:

1   Emotional skills – to help us maintain control over both the quantity and quality of our feelings.
2   Communication skills – to help us assert and promote ourselves and our ideas and protect ourselves from unhelpful criticism.
3   Organizational skills – to help us use our and others' time, energy and skills efficiently and effectively.

We must ensure that each and every one of these skills is in superlative shape if we want to maintain momentum, and manage even the roughest of life's roads. Let me tell you a 'Jack and Jill' story which I hope will inspire you!

You will notice that in the text of my story I have highlighted a number of words. These are the ones which are relevant to our Success from Setbacks work.

Jill is the owner and manager of a small but highly successful marketing company. She has devoted the past 10 years of her life to this enterprise, and now she is justly proud of her achievement in building up the business in an area which had previously been very mistrustful of her profession.

Last week her team heard that a well-known multinational firm had opened an office in the town. Jill is now understandably anxious. Not only is there a danger that this company will poach much of the business she has built up over several years, she is also very afraid that she is going to lose her best staff to this firm. These are people that she has trained and nurtured for many years. Even though many are now close friends, she knows that they will be tempted by the security and money that this firm can offer.

But Jill has a kitbag full of Thriver qualities, so:

- she is determined not to sink into despair - she **trusts** that there will be a solution. She uses her **humility** to seek out support and advice from other people she knows have survived this kind of setback. She is **resolutely** determined to keep afloat. Not surprisingly, she then has an **ingenious** idea for developing a new niche market which her competitor is highly unlikely to be able to enter. She knows that she has the **versatility** to adapt to the new situation, and that she can keep the business working **efficiently** even in the atmosphere of panic this news has brought. She doesn't sit and moan about the injustices of the Global Goliaths gorging on the hard, pioneering work of innovative small businesses. She takes **responsibility** for finding a solution to the problem.

She calls her staff to a meeting to discuss their strategy.

Unfortunately, Jack, her highly talented senior project manager, is in no mood for such a meeting. He's had a bad night at home. One of his children smashed the neighbour's patio door during an over-enthusiastic game of pavement tennis. His wife seized upon the crisis to bombard him with his fatherly failings and their mounting overdraft.

Presenting the unwelcome facts, Jill **tentatively** starts to **promote** her new idea. She notices Jack sneering, she is taken aback and begins to fumble with her words. Jack seizes the moment: This is an ideal opportunity to get his own back on the world (especially a female member of it!). He is so much more articulate and financially astute than Jill. He begins to demolish and ridicule her 'so-called plan'.

His unfair reaction proves to be one too many setbacks for Jill's 'Personal Skill Wheel' to bear. She is hurt and finds herself **speechless**. She **doesn't know how to assert herself** in the face of his put-downs and destructive criticism. She has never met with such an outright aggressive response before. **Tears well up** in her eyes, which only makes Jack's bullying accelerate. He attacks her for bringing up the idea without having **consulted the team**, **prepared a realistic budget**, or **developed a workable strategy**.

Then Jill's **anger flares**. She bangs her file on the table and walks out, saying Jack had better send off an application to 'Global Giant'.

Jack does, and Jill is left with yet another setback on her plate!

Fortunately, however, my story doesn't end here. It has a happy ending: Jill's newly strengthened humility and trust come to her rescue. She first rings her local bookshop and orders a book on assertiveness, another on managing anger, and then she rings her accountant and asks for help with preparing a business plan for her new idea.

Three years on, Jill's marketing company is still there and still flourishing. It is now such a thorn in the side of Global Giant that they are considering making her an offer she certainly won't *want* to refuse! She is, quite unexpectedly, destined for a lifetime of financial security. Meanwhile, our embittered villain Jack still sweats and toils and no longer has a wife to mop his brow!

I hope most of you were able to see the point of this morality tale! But, as there may be some of you who may still need convincing, let me elaborate the point a little further.

In spite of all Jill's wonderful Thriver qualities, she failed at first to make a success out of her setback because:

- She did not *promote her idea in a confident, authoritative manner.* This is the most appropriate communication style for a leader in most anxiety-provoking setback situations.
- She did not have *good enough emotional skills to be able to control her emotional responses* to Jack's disloyal, unsupportive and unfair aggression. The result was that Jill found herself feeling and behaving like a victim, even though she did not want to do so.
- She did not have the assertive skills *to protect herself and stop the flow of Jack's put-downs and destructive criticism*, so he continued until she *became too angry to stay in command of the situation* and lost a talented, experienced member of staff when she could least afford to do so.

> Under the stress of setbacks, we must always be ready and waiting for difficult behaviour to emerge from all sorts of unexpected sources.

I hope you noticed that, in our story, Jill did not *depend* on a change in Jack's attitude or behaviour before making a success from her setback. She *took responsibility for her own failings and seized an opportunity for her own growth.*

To return to our metaphor, Jill noticed her Skills Wheel was weak and took immediate steps to make sure that it could be strengthened. She accepted the limitations of her power. She knew that she could do very little to stop Global Giant from placing boulders in her tracks and that she could not wave a magic personal development wand over Jack. But she did what was possible. She learned new skills which at least ensured that she could respond more constructively should she meet either kind of setback again.

In order to make a success from setbacks, we must:

> ... Accept the things which cannot be changed,
> have the courage to change the things that we want to change
> and have the wisdom to distinguish one from the other
> ADAPTED FROM 'THE SERENITY PRAYER' ATTRIBUTED
> TO REINHOLD NIEBUHR, 1943

Before leaving this tale, I'd like to say that I do not believe the Jacks of the world should be dismissed as lost causes. They *can* change, but the reality is that during the heat of a crisis, it may not be *your* priority to help them, and they may not be in the mood to admit that they need to do so! In Jill's position, an achievable goal would have been to curb Jack's bullying behaviour with a more assertive and emotionally-controlled response. At a later date, she could have confronted him with his share of the problem and advised him to do some training in emotional management and assertiveness. And if he had done so he might have lived more happily ever after!

The range of personal skills we may need to call upon to deal with setbacks is very wide. Jill's story illustrates the need for certain kinds, but there are also other ones which may be just as essential.

- If we are feeling disappointed at a poor exam result, or sad because a much-loved pet has died, we need to be skilled at *emotional healing* so we can put the past behind us and begin to look positively to the future.
- If we are feeling frustrated because a part that we were expecting to arrive for a broken machine has not turned

up, we need to be *skilled at writing an assertive letter of complaint.*

- If a deadline has been unexpectedly moved forward, we need the skills to be able to reorganize our *action plan* ourselves quickly and make *rapid decisions.*
- If other people have 'gone quiet' in response to the panic they feel during a setback, we need *active listening* skills to help them articulate their needs.
- If we have made a mistake, we need to know how to control our nagging *guilt.*
- If we have lost money over the setback, we need *budgeting* skills to get us back onto a sound financial track.
- If we need to encourage new customers to buy our wares, we will need *presentation skills.*
- If our setback has put such pressure on us that we now need to work more closely with other people to find a solution, we need *teamwork* skills.
- If we need to risk failing, we need to *control our fear* of this and know how to create and implement effective *contingency planning.*
- If we need to persuade others to give us a second (or third) chance, we need to be skilled at *self-promotion.*

When we read (or write!) a list like this, it seems glaringly obvious that personal skills play a crucial role in determining our chance of becoming both successful and happy. But the reality is that most people have had very little help in learning to acquire them. Up until about 15 years ago, not only were such skills underrated in terms of their power, they were barely recognized as being skills at all. It was thought that we were either blessed or not with the 'gifts' from Mother Nature which helped us, for example, to keep our cool or be 'pushy' or decisive under the pressure of a setback.

With the advent of social science research, we now know that these 'gifts' are in fact learned knowledge and behavioural habits, which can be acquired. If we have inherited a thin, buckled Wheel, we can reinforce it or even change it!

In Chapter 8 I have selected some of the key techniques, strategies and guidelines I have found particularly useful for dealing with setbacks. But please remember the few I have chosen to include in this book are only an introduction. There are many more to be learned. Some of you may be lucky enough to have access to this kind of training through your work. If you have, seize every opportunity to go on courses and to suggest different ones to your training department if you need them. Other people may need to seek out their own courses privately or use self-help books and cassettes. At the end of each of the next three sections, you will see that I have included a few suggestions to at least start you thinking in a practical way about the action you could resolve to take.

Emotional Skills

Setbacks are a great test of our emotional skills. People who are:

- normally calm and controlled in their everyday life can suddenly become unrecognizably histrionic and volatile
- generally cheerful and spirited can become engulfed in apathy and despair
- usually excited about new challenges become fearful of doing mundane chores well within their capability.

Why does this happen? A very basic understanding of how our emotional system works might help to explain.

Our brain has two main centres which produce our feelings. One is used for our everyday life and the other for emergency situations. The first uses our sophisticated thinking brain, the neocortex, to analyse what is happening in the world around us, and then produce a tailor-made emotional response to each new situation. The second uses a more primitive, crude centre called the amygdala to initiate an instant, pre-programmed response. These responses are blueprints for action which have been inherited from previous generations, or were imprinted on our brain during our impressionable childhood years. They are crude responses which are essentially designed to prepare us physically for either fighting or fleeing.

It is the second response which tends to take control during the crisis of a setback. The problem is that feelings which are generated by the blueprint are often inappropriate to the complexities of our modern adult problems. We therefore find ourselves experiencing feelings which we and others may consider childish or inappropriate, irrational or simply 'over-the-top'.

In our story, Jill responded to the shock of Jack's attack (fight response) by becoming 'speechless' and producing tears (fleeing responses). Under further attack, her auto-pilot switched her into uncontrolled anger (fight response). If both Jack and Jill had been more emotionally skilled, they would have been aware that they were responding inappropriately, and they could have used a technique to control their emotional emergency system and respond to each other in an assertive rather than a passive (fleeing) or aggressive (fighting) manner. If they had, *maybe* our story would have had a different ending. Perhaps, working co-operatively together, they could have produced an even better idea and maybe Jack might have found in Jill a supportive, listening ear. There can be no guarantee that this would have happened, of course, but in my experience if crises like these are handled in an emotionally skilled way, win/win solutions are much more likely to emerge.

In Chapter 8 you will find a few of my own favourite techniques which can be used to switch ourselves into the emotional state which we (and not the caveman or child within us) *think* will cope best with the setback we are facing.

SUGGESTIONS FOR FURTHER HELP

● Buy or borrow other self-help books on the subject (the Further Reading List beginning on page 186 has just a tiny fraction of the ones which I could recommend. But don't consult me on the subject, I'm prejudiced! Ask an expert specialist bookseller for advice).

- Consult a counsellor or join a self-help group.
- Join a class in relaxation or yoga (or start up a group of your own at work or in your community).
- Join a gym or do some other form of aerobic or stretching exercises (daily!).
- Learn to meditate – it is much easier than you think, and you don't have to be religious to use the techniques. (Many people find it easier to do this in a class, though it works just as well doing it on your own.)
- Buy (and listen regularly to!) relaxing CDs and tapes.
- Learn about aromatherapy and how it can be used to both suppress and lift your mood. (Scents are reputed to have the quickest route to the emotional brain. This is probably because we had 'nose brains' before we evolved any of our other more intellectual functions!)

> Serenity comes not alone by removing the outward causes and occasions of fear, but by the discovery of inward reservoirs to draw upon.
>
> RUFUS M. JONES

JUNG CHANG

Jung Chang is the author of the international best-selling family history *Wild Swans.* Her book graphically depicts life in revolutionary China. For the first time, it made many millions of people aware of the reality of life for ordinary people under the regimes of that period. She herself endured a childhood of unbelievable hardship and terror, seeing her parents tormented and interned in camps. She did not see her first foreigner until she was 23. Against many odds, she won a scholarship to study in England and became the first person from China to receive a British doctorate.

Communication Skills

If you happened to be riding along a very smooth, familiar path in life, you could, arguably, skip this section. For example, if your journey was taking you around a small, intimate, peaceful community, you could easily get by with minimal communication skills.

- You wouldn't need to sell yourself to find a job. People would already know through the grapevine about your strengths, and they wouldn't need an impressive CV to convince them of your suitability for the job.
- You'd have no need for the current chat-up lines, because your potential partner may well have been to infant school with you, and had his or her eye on you ever since and you would live happily ever after together for the rest of your lives.
- You wouldn't need the 'gift of the gab' to promote your new product or service. People would be more than willing to buy it because they would probably be loyal customers already and you would, of course, have no other competitors.
- You wouldn't have to know how to untangle 'crossed wires' when having a debate with your neighbours about how to rebuild your broken shared fence, because your discussions would always stay on the same easy wavelength.
- Nor would you have to know how to write a punchy complaint letter, because you would have nothing to complain about!

But I guess if you are reading this book your journey hasn't proved quite this easy! You are probably living in the real world! Like me you inhabit this vast global community where it is becoming increasingly difficult for individuals to make their unique voice heard and understood. This is indeed a world in which Thrivers need to have not just good-enough, but *excellent* communication skills.

I have included some guidelines and strategies in the Strategies chapter (beginning on page 151).

SUGGESTIONS FOR FURTHER HELP

- Enrol on one of the many courses now available in specific areas of communication (such as Presentation Skills, Effective Listening, Persuasive Skills, Body Language, Cross-cultural Communication, etc.). These are probably the best way to learn these skills, because they offer practice and can help you to obtain honest, confrontative feedback.
- Buy or borrow books on the above subjects and practise the exercises with a friend (see Further Reading).
- Record good communicators on the TV and radio. Use these recordings to help you study their technique. Watch their body language; note how they listen and argue; note the kind of language they use to make persuasive points and protect themselves from difficult questions and put-downs.
- Treat yourself to a session with an image consultant. (Research has shown that 55 per cent of the impact of a first impression is made through dress. First impressions last!)
- Enrol for some voice training or join a local drama group that coaches its members in voice projection and inflection.
- Listen to 'books on tape' read by actors with excellent voices.
- Join a debating group (or, indeed, a pressure group which is constantly arguing about issues and projects!).

ELEANOR ROOSEVELT 1884–1962

Eleanor was the wife of President Franklin Roosevelt. Before she was 10 her parents and brother had died. Her childhood was lonely and unhappy until she was sent away to school in

England at the age of 15, when her confidence was first nurtured by a teacher. During her years as the president's wife, her personal life was often very stressful. Two of her children died in infancy, her husband developed polio and was known to be regularly unfaithful in spite of his condition. Throughout, Eleanor maintained an independent working life, becoming one of America's greatest social reformers. After her husband's death she became chair of the Commission on Human Rights. She played an influential part in the formulation of the Universal Declaration of Human Rights.

Organizational Skills

> Making a success out of something has nothing to do with luck. Care, thought, and study go into making something succeed; luck is something you get when playing the lottery, a roulette game or gambling.
>
> WESS ROBERTS

Although I *feel* that this is an area of great weakness for me, I am always being told how well organized I am. So eventually I have been convinced that my level of organizational skills must be at least above average. In my day-to-day life, however, this conviction has little impact. I am too preoccupied with thoughts about how much easier my life would be and how much more I could achieve if I was even better organized! (It is hard to please a naturally disorganized perfectionist!)

But in the wake of a setback, I have to admit that these self-doubts disappear. I start to brim with confidence in my ability to manage my way out of the problem. In crisis situations that demand action, it is my efficient, down-to-earth planning that is praised more often than my other traits such as sensitivity and creativity, which I know are more central to my character.

One of the ways I have helped myself become more organized is to devise *strategies*. These strategies are often similar to those you might find in management books, but they also have a personal development component designed *to keep me psychologically on track*. They can, of course, be used to help you become more organized at home as well as in the office. I have included some of my favourite ones in the Strategies chapter (pages 165–177).

SUGGESTIONS FOR FURTHER HELP

- Visit the management or business section of your library or bookshop. There are now so many books on this subject you could save a good deal of time by asking for some guidance on where to start looking, but I have found that there is nothing to beat a good hour's browsing – so choose one that has a café on site! (Also see the Further Reading chapter.)
- Enrol on a time-management course.
- Treat yourself to some new toys! Take a visit to an office equipment superstore and buy some new 'tools' to help you organize your office either at home or at work. Perhaps a superbly designed filing tray or colourful paper clips may inspire you into renewed efficiency. (It works for me, if only temporarily!)
- Ask several friends who are highly organized for tips. List these in your diary and try one tip per week for a few months.
- If you have the time, money and aptitude, do an MBA (Masters degree in Business Administration)!
- Send off for the short course prospectus of local Management and Business Schools, and practise your assertive skills to then persuade your boss to invest in sending you on one!
- Suggest that the company you work for employs the services of a management consultancy. While they are on site, pick their brains for your personal use!
- Treat yourself to some private individual sessions with a mentor or coach who specializes in this area.

INSTANT WORKOUT

Turn to pages 165–177 in the chapter on Strategies. Read through at least the headings of each, and note which of these could be useful for you to either learn or revise.

Select three to focus on during the next month.

1 _____

2 _____

3 _____

> One cannot get through life without pain ... what we can do is choose how to use the pain life presents to us.
>
> BERNIE S. SIEGAL

AUGUSTE RODIN 1840–1917

The French sculptor Rodin was born into a poor family, and although he was known to be talented at drawing from an early age, he failed the entrance exams to art school. He started to earn a living doing decorative stonework and so became a sculptor. He was rejected many times for competitions for monuments, and did not achieve any commissions for very many years. When he did start producing his masterpieces, they were often severely criticized by the art establishment. Nevertheless, he persevered and became a sculptor of international acclaim and has a museum in Paris devoted entirely to his work.

CHAPTER 3

Wheel 2: Fitness Programmes for Body, Mind and Spirit

> When the going gets tough, the tough get going.
>
> JOSEPH P. KENNEDY

Setbacks have a nasty habit of highlighting any lurking weakness not only in our bodies but in our minds and spirits as well. So now we are going to turn our attention to strengthening the three sections of our *Fitness* Wheel.

I cannot pretend to be a paragon of virtue in any of these areas. Even the sound of the word 'fitness' sends shivers of guilt through my body! But I don't want rescuing from these uncomfortable feelings. I have found that there isn't much comfort to be had from knowing that I am not alone in my shaking. In fact, my anxieties increase when I hear others trying to pardon my 'sins of omission' by sharing their guilty secrets.

Does it depress or comfort you to hear someone respond to your guilty confessions with comments like these?

> 'Oh, yes, I've joined gyms many times and never go.'
> 'I know, I shouldn't be driving there either – it's an easy walk.'
> 'Oh, yes, I am like that – always meaning to sign up for adult education classes and then making the excuse that there is no time.'
> 'I bet you can remember more than I can – my brain is rusting up.'
> 'Yes, I love reading, but I haven't read a novel in years either.'
> 'Yes, I went to Rome last year – as you say, all you get round to seeing is the inside of the conference centre.'

Although I am not searching for saints as friends, I don't want others to share these kinds of weaknesses. I would rather be living in a world inhabited by people who are disciplined and motivated enough to stick to fitness schedules which they set for their bodies, minds and souls. My reasons are primarily very selfish. First, I find such people more inspiring to be with, and secondly, it is comforting to know that their strength would be there to support and rescue me should I meet a setback I cannot manage alone.

Recently I was reflecting on the value of the help I received after the death of my daughter, and became very aware that *during that major crisis I needed people whose physical stamina could match the pace, whose minds responded with speed and agility, and whose own inner spiritual strength could withstand being battered by my anguish and despair.* Ideally, in *lesser crises*, when we have to be or are expected to be self-reliant, we should be able to draw on these same resources *from within ourselves.* In today's highly pressurized world few of us can take our strengths in any of these areas for granted. In order to ensure our fitness in all three areas, we should check ourselves regularly and take *toning actions* as soon as we spot a weakness occurring. The next three sections are designed to help you to do just this. You will notice that they vary in the length of their content. This is no reflection of their relative importance. It is merely because in the physical fitness area my professional expertise is so limited that I am sure you would be better served by professional advice from someone in that field. In the area of mind fitness, although I have more (but still limited) expertise, I have already covered the subject in other books. In the spiritual area, however, I have developed some new ideas which I thought would be useful to share in more length because they have evolved directly from helping myself and so many others recover from dispiriting setbacks.

Physical Fitness

Few of us need to be preached at on this subject anymore. In recent years we have been bombarded (quite rightly, of course!) with every conceivable variety of health campaign. We know what we *should* do, but most of us are still finding it hard either to kick the bad habits of a lifetime or resist the temptations of sloth and certain 'naughty' sensual pleasures. If you want to try yet another tool to help you become as physically fit as you are able, try using the following self-questionnaire from time to time.

Give yourself a rating on a 1–10 scale over the past week. I have included some suggestions, but remember my expertise is very limited and there are plenty more to be had from the real experts.

AEROBIC EXERCISE

The latest research suggests that this should be at least *three 20-minute periods* per week. It should be the kind of exercise which makes you sweat a little and your heart and lungs work noticeably harder, so that you are slightly out of breath.

- Change your routine if you find you do not stick to it.
- Take notice of the exercise which is working for you rather than for other people around you, or what happens to be fashionable at the moment.
- Find regular, easy ways to do the kind of exercise which can become *automatic*; for example, habits such as taking the stairs instead of the lift.
- Buy (or borrow!) a lively dog (the only method guaranteed to get me moving fast enough!).

STRETCH EXERCISES

A quick tension-releasing form of these should be done *every hour of the day* if you have a sedentary job. Other more lengthy regimes should be done to suit your individual needs and age as often as you have been advised to do them. (I now have to do 20 minutes each morning to prevent back, neck and various other aches from becoming distracting pains!).

- Make a habit (like the cat!) of doing 5–10 minutes' gentle stretching before getting out of bed.
- If you have a sedentary job, get up and stretch your body every hour.
- Treat yourself to a stretch from a professional from time to time (e.g. a physiotherapist, an osteopath, chiropractor, remedial masseur).
- Take up yoga or a stretch class.

STRENGTHENING EXERCISES

Find out what muscles *you* really need to be dependably strong and make sure these are strengthened by appropriate exercise *at least three times a week*. (The Thriver is more concerned with brawn than beauty!)

- Two bags of potatoes or sugar make good substitutes for weights (tip from a personal trainer!).

- You can do many of these while standing around because of a setback. For example, if you find yourself waiting for a delayed plane – use your bags for weights, but make sure that they are evenly weighted. (Of course, you would never carry them *anywhere,* any other way, would you?!)

DIET

This should of course always be highly nutritious and well balanced, but we should take even greater care during periods of increased pressure when our bodies use up more energy.

- Always cut down on toxins such as caffeine and alcohol during times of setbacks.
- Save the diets (if you have to have them) for the quiet patches in your life.
- Drink 2 litres of good quality water a day – you may need more if you are in a hotter country than the UK. Water is essential for the brain and is the best detoxifier, and it should be cheap!
- Consult one of the latest books on the biochemistry of food, and eat the foods which you need for your lifestyle and body. New research is emerging all the time. One theory is that people with different blood groups require different diets. Use this kind of research to motivate you to eat better, but stop reading the moment it starts to make you anxious, and *don't* lend your books to anyone with an eating disorder, *especially* if they are experiencing a setback.

SLEEP

You should be having early nights and peaceful dreams!

- Take regular cat-naps during the day. A short rest or sleep eight hours after waking is recommended for most people.
- Watch and respect your biorhythms. Be active during your 'up' cycles and rest during your low periods. Buy or

borrow a book on the subject if you want to know more.
(See Further Reading.)

RELAXATION

Taking the body into a state of *deep* relaxation is reputed to be
even more beneficial than sleep for healing and repair purposes.

- Do a deep relaxation at least once a day. For ideas and
  exercises see pages 151–154.
- Treat yourself to a weekly massage or Turkish bath or
  something similar during times of extreme pressure.

FRESH AIR

Oxygen feeds the brain as well as the muscles.

- Try to sleep with your window open at night if you are
  indoors most of the day.
- Thrivers need good quality air-conditioning if that's the
  air they have to breathe. Check yours is functioning
  efficiently and that the filters are changed frequently. (And
  remember, you have a right to know about your system at
  work.)
- Plants in your rooms will help, but some are better than
  others. Consult a gardener or garden centre for advice.
- Buy an ionizer or air filter machine especially if you live or
  work in a smoky or a dusty atmosphere.

PROBLEM AREA MAINTENANCE

This should include anything you know you are supposed to
do to keep one or more of your physical weaknesses in check
(e.g. my husband has to moisturize his skin to keep his problematic skin from drying out).

- Go for regular check-ups.
- Get to know your family's medical history and pay special attention to the areas where you may have a genetically inherited weakness *before* any symptoms emerge.

Instant Exercise

Turn to page 165 and use the Positive Action Strategy to plan a physical fitness programme for yourself to improve at least one of the above areas.

GERI HALLIWELL 1972–

Geri was one of the founder members of the record-breaking singing group, the Spice Girls. Her childhood and early adulthood were tough and poverty stricken. The death of her father was a major trauma, but she dealt with it by throwing herself into her work with the group. In the space of five years Geri progressed from being homeless and socially wayward, to becoming a United Nations goodwill ambassador after leaving the Spice Girls at the age of 26. She believes that a reason for her success was that 'nothing was handed to me on a plate. I'm glad I've been through what I have – it made me grow.'

Mind Fitness

> As a man thinks, so he does become.
> MIGUEL DE CERVANTES

Have you ever had the experience of being so stunned by a setback that your mind has gone totally blank?

If you haven't, I am sure you must have had one or more of these experiences:

- not being able to 'think straight'
- having the same thoughts whirling around your head in everlasting circles

- finding you can no longer do the simplest calculations
- finding you cannot remember phone numbers or someone's name
- not being able to concentrate on reading or listening to music
- not being able to understand a simple plot or set of instructions
- forgetting how to do simple tasks (e.g. when you absent-mindedly put the tea in the fridge instead of the teapot!)
- seeing mental visions of doom-laden scenarios
- hearing unhelpful, critical 'voices' in your head.

When we are desperate to find a solution to our setback, these kinds of experiences are at best annoying and at worst terrifying or enraging. Fortunately, for me these internal setbacks in my head no longer take me in their grip for long. But I can still vividly recall the days when they used to do so. I'm glad I haven't forgotten, because it helps me to understand many of my clients who report having been in this kind of mental state for many months before coming to see me.

Of course, we cannot completely prevent major crises having this kind of impact, but I am convinced that developing mind fitness can stop it from happening so regularly, and enable us to recover control if we do notice a functioning problem.

Unfortunately, compared to our knowledge of the body, our knowledge of the mind is still severely limited. But the good news is that we are currently living in the most exciting times in the history of humankind with respect to our understanding of the brain. Very soon we shall know so much more about this area of fitness.

But if you want to do more than sit and watch the adventure unfold, you can start developing your strengths in the areas of mind functioning that can help us cope better with setbacks.

> The adventure is only just beginning.
> SUSAN GREENFIELD, *THE HUMAN BRAIN - A GUIDED TOUR*

Here are suggestions to start you thinking of what you may

be able to do. To maintain your mind in a fit, healthy and agile state, make sure that it is fed with enough of the following:

POSITIVE VISUALIZATIONS

We now know that creating pictures of successful outcomes in our minds can energize our mind and help it stay focused on what *we* want to do.

- Do creative visualizations regularly.
- Describe your vision to others in graphic detail.
- Draw your vision, or a symbol of it, and keep it pinned up somewhere.
- Pin up inspiring quotes such as this one:

> The mind is its own place, and in itself
> Can make a Heav'n of Hell, and a Hell of Heav'n
>
> JOHN MILTON

CONCEPTUAL CHALLENGES

After a setback we may need to look at situations and issues differently.

- Seize opportunities for heated arguments with people who challenge your thinking approach.
- Join a debating group.
- Read books on theories such as evolution, Big Bang and religion.

> You have to move up to another level of thinking, which is true for me and everybody else. Everybody has to learn to think differently, bigger, to be open to possibilities.
>
> OPRAH WINFREY

ANALYTICAL PRACTICE

Most setbacks present us with at least one problem to solve.

- Join an adult education class which will give you opportunities to do this.

- Learn the Joint Problem Solving Strategy on page 175–177.
- Watch political debates on TV.

LOGIC TRAINING

To stop your mind from 'wandering all over the place' you must develop the skill of being able to switch it into logical mode. Make sure your left brain is well exercised.

- Buy puzzle books for train journeys instead of a newspaper sometimes.
- Join a philosophy or maths evening class.
- Go on a computer course.
- Watch court dramas on TV or at the cinema.
- Read detective stories.

ARITHMETICAL PRACTICE

You may not have your calculator or accountant handy in every setback situation.

- If you are going abroad, don't pack the 'ready reckoner' for working out currency exchange rates.
- When you are sitting in traffic jams, give yourself mini-arithmetical tests such as: *how many days/hours/minutes(!) is it since I set off/got married/was born(!)?* or, *If I were to travel at the average speed achieved on this journey so far, how long would it take me to get to London/Madrid?*
- Occasionally try to add up your supermarket bill as you put your goods on the belt by the till.

MEMORY TRAINING

No one's memory works as well when they are anxious and fearful, so you may need to give it some extra support.

- Buy yourself a memory-training book which will teach you visualization techniques (e.g. attributing a symbolic picture of an object to numbers, and making up stories around these images to remember number sequences).

- Get into the habit of repeating the name of a new acquaintance several times in the first 20 minutes of meeting them. (Research indicates that if we remember something for this length of time, it is much more likely to 'stick' in our mind.)
- Before looking up a telephone number in your address book, get into the habit of trying to recall it from your mind's memory store.
- Fan the flames of your emotions when trying to memorize something important. If you are excited when you see a new face you are more likely to remember it; if you summon up enthusiasm for a treat to have when you have finished your revision, the facts are more likely to stick.

CONCENTRATION EXERCISES

In setback situations we often don't have the luxury of perfect peace and quiet. We have to be able to concentrate in spite of the chaos going on around us.

- Practise reading and working in busy and noisy situations. Start with very short concentration spans and then gradually increase them.
- Learn speed-reading techniques such as running a pencil tip under the words as you read them.
- Learn meditation.

CREATIVITY DEVELOPMENT

Earlier we noted how important it is in many setback situations to come up with new solutions, or at the very least with variations on the themes of an old approach. For some people this will always be easier to do than for others, but we all have a measure of creativity, and what we have can be developed through exercise.

- Take up a creative style of hobby such as art, creative writing or a craft which involves coming up with new ideas or ways of doing things.
- Encourage suggestion boxes at work and prizes for good ideas.
- Develop the habit of Brainstorming before settling down to writing or planning any project (see page 183).
- Use Mind Maps for note-taking and planning notes (see page 184).
- Do a meditation when you need to switch into right-brain mode.
- Use symbols to help you identify and remember things (this will help to fix them in your memory while stimulating your creative juices).
- Treat yourself to a Flotation from time to time. Floating is deeply relaxing and reputed to stimulate creativity (special Flotation tanks can be found in some health and relaxation centres – you basically float for 30–60 minutes in warm water with Dead Sea salts or on a specially-built flotation bed. You can be in total darkness or very subdued light.) Alternatively, go floating in a quiet swimming pool or warm sea.

> Everything starts as somebody's daydream.
>
> LARRY NIVEN

CROSS-LATERAL EXERCISING

For problem-solving in setback situations we often need to be able to switch back and forth quickly and smoothly from our right (emotional and creative) to our left (logical) brain functioning modes.

- Do Brain Gym exercises (see page 181).

MONITORING YOUR UNCONSCIOUS

The anxiety we may feel during a setback can bring up old anxieties and prejudices and out-of-date, programmed beliefs (e.g. those belonging to your parents or based on gender stereotyping). Keep an eye on what is happening in your unconscious mind.

- Record your dreams in a book and look for patterns and recurring themes which may indicate unconscious worries.
- Attend guided meditation workshops which encourage unconscious thoughts to come to the surface.
- Ask assertive friends to give you honest feedback when you indicate a prejudice (we all have them!).
- Visit a hypnotist or psychoanalyst.

> Freedom is what you do with what has been done to you.
>
> JEAN PAUL SARTRE

EMOTIONAL SPOT-CHECKS

Out-of-control emotions (negative or positive) can severely hamper our ability to think clearly.

- Practise your emotional skills (see pages 151–155).
- Make a habit of asking yourself what you are feeling (not thinking) every so often.
- Become aware of signs in your body and behaviour which may indicate that you are in an emotional state without you realizing it. For example:
  - Not reading the daily paper may be a sign that you are in a state of apathy and your thinking is likely to be running slow. You may need to do some aerobic exercise or a positive visualization.
  - Butterflies in your stomach may indicate over-excitement. You may need to do some relaxation to quiet the butterflies in your mind.
- Ask friends to give you feedback when you are showing non-verbal signs of repressed feeling (e.g. tapping a table with a pen while smiling; talking positively but with a worried brow; looking at your watch while 'pretending' to listen).

> Our life is what our thoughts make of it.
>
> MARCUS AURELIUS

JACK ASHLEY 1922–

Jack left school at 14 years old. He became a labourer but worked his way through college, earning himself scholarships to both Oxford and Cambridge Universities. At the start of his political career a minor operation to his ear went wrong and he became deaf. Throughout his career he has continued to be a staunch and highly successful champion for many kinds of disabled groups.

Spiritual Fitness

I cannot have enough reminders about how important this area of fitness is, especially after a setback. This is certainly not because I believe it is of lesser importance than the other areas. It is because I know only too well how it has a tendency to slip down my list of priorities whenever I am in a state of stress.

But, of course, if ever there is a time when my spirit needs a boost, it is after a setback. When this part of me is strong, my self-esteem is buoyant and I have enduring faith in my ability to find a happy, balanced and fulfilling life once again.

Perhaps before I go any further I should explain the meaning I am attributing to the word 'spirit' for the purposes of this section. Like many others before me I find this particularly hard to do. How can a mere mortal describe the indescribable?!

My interpretation (and not necessarily *anyone* else's) covers aspects of a human being which include:

- the parts of them which have no material form (at least to our human eye) and are often referred to as their 'soul'
- their unique fundamental nature – the element which comes into being the moment they are conceived (though one day I may be convinced it is also there before conception)
- their force or presence which continues to exist after the death of their body
- their moral and intellectual essence (the individual personal pattern created by their beliefs and values)
- the component of their individual energy which is connected to the universal life-force
- their own distinctive 'aura' which is present in the atmosphere which surrounds them when you are in their company.

I am well aware that this interpretation will not be shared by everyone. It may be particularly disputed by people who have a religion which defines the concepts of 'spirit' and 'soul' more distinctly. I hope, however, that you have at least a 'good-enough' understanding to be able to read this section, because I am convinced that the spiritual part of ourselves does exist, needs nurturing to keep it healthy, and we need it to be in good shape to be able to make a success from a setback.

In the English language, we commonly refer to a nurturing process as 'feeding the soul'. So I thought I would also use the metaphor of food to describe the elements which I believe our spirit needs in order to become, or remain, 'fit' enough to support a Thriver.

For the last few years I have been giving this subject a good deal of thought and noting and observing exactly which kinds of 'foods' seem to be feeding my own and others' spirits. I have also been reading as extensively as I can on the subject. Earlier this year I forced myself to clarify and summarize this learning by offering to do a talk on the subject. The result was that I found that I could identify 12 specific kinds of 'staple foods for the soul'. Most of these are provided by the rituals and practices of most traditional religions, but can also be obtained in a secular form by participating in certain 'everyday' activities. This means that even the most 'heathen' among us now has no excuse for not having a robust and stalwart spirit!

An important point to remember about these special 'foods' is that *their storage life is limited, and that, ideally, we should be 'drip fed' with a balanced diet of the whole range*. It is not therefore sufficient to give yourself a bumper top-up of one or two foods once a year while on holiday. We need to make a habit of giving ourselves regular small doses as well, even if that means making a slight detour off the direct route on our journey to our goals. If you are like me, you will have to remind yourself that you will return refreshed and remotivated and will probably arrive at the end of your journey more, rather than less, speedily. And that even if you do take a little longer, you will not be burnt out and will be much more able to keep 'cycling' at a Thriver's pace for the rest of your life.

So the next section will help you to check on how well you are *currently* feeding your spirit. It can also be used after each setback, to ensure that you do not neglect this important aspect of yourself at a time when you need it most.

THE 10 FOODS FOR THE SPIRIT

As you read each individual section ask yourself:

- How many minutes or hours have I spent giving myself some of this 'food' during the last week?
- Was this an adequate amount of time? (Don't forget that after a setback we have a tendency to become dispirited, so we need more, not less of these 'foods'.)
- What will I be doing next week to give myself this 'food'?

Please note: the 'foods' are not listed in any order of importance. We need them all! You may notice that some of my suggestions for obtaining them are duplicated under various headings. I have done this to reinforce the point that often in the process of doing one activity, we find it gives us several kinds of spiritual food. So in the coming few weeks, watch out for the ones which yield a bumper crop – they are obviously the ones to concentrate on after a setback!

Spirit Food 1: Sanctuary

This food should give us some *peace and quiet*. We need to give ourselves time in a safe, sheltered environment in which we can *reflect* and do what is commonly called some *'soul-searching'*.

As our world becomes more and more crowded and noisy, more and more people are yearning for this food. But sadly they often start to act in response to their yearning only when their spirits have become seriously depleted, they are feeling physically 'stressed-out' and their mind is whirring uncontrollably around in circles.

Thrivers make sure that they rarely reach this state of mind and body before seeking sanctuary. They know that when they have reached this stage it is in fact very hard to take advantage of its recuperative powers. This is why so many people become disenchanted. They may pay vast sums of money to find sanctuary on a deserted beach or country hide-away, but find they cannot switch off. They tell me that the peace and quiet in fact makes them feel even more panicky, because it is so strange and unfamiliar. They spend their time worrying about the negative aspects of their setback, and resenting taking time away from their problems.

The aim of the Thriver is to make their special places of sanctuary so familiar that their emotional brain makes an instant recognition and orders the body and the mind to relax instantly. If you visit your sanctuaries *frequently*, you may even save time in the long run. This is because you will be able to use every moment in *useful* reflection or meditation, and can return to your problems re-energized, having taken less time to solve them.

So, although I am certainly not against wonderfully long extended breaks in peaceful locations, we should aim at taking them

> Make a habit of finding the time and space (and suitable places) to have Sanctuary in your life *every day.*

by choice and not out of necessity. If we wait until we *need* to go to places like this, we are less likely to be in good enough shape to enjoy them!

Suggestions for Finding Sanctuary

- Take a relaxing bath instead of a rushed shower at least three times a week.
- Learn simple quick meditation techniques and practise these for 5 minutes each day.
- When standing in a queue, take four or five deep slow breaths and then use your imagination to take you mentally to one of your favourite peaceful spots.
- Put your alarm on 10 minutes earlier, especially when you know you have a busy day ahead. Wake and dress yourself as usual, but spend 10 minutes quietly contemplating on your bed before starting your day. Think about the aspects of the day you *are* looking forward to (not worrying about!).
- Take 10 minutes at the end of each day, listening to relaxing music. (If you must do some chores, wear a Walkman!).
- Make a habit of popping into a church for 5 minutes' peace and contemplation whenever you are passing (you can do this even if you are not religious, and most will welcome you, especially if you donate a small amount to the upkeep fund).
- Make another habit of spending at least 5 minutes a day in a garden or park.
- Buy some tapes of natural sounds (lapping waves, the rainforest, etc.) and take these, an eye shade and your Walkman whenever you are travelling by crowded, noisy public transport. These sounds are sometimes better for contemplation than using music which can be distracting.
- Keep a journal (it doesn't have to be written daily). Use it to jot down anything that comes into your mind – don't attempt to make it a literary work or a documentary recording of the day (you can keep a separate book if you want to do either of these).

Spirit Food 2: Intimacy

This food is obtained from spending *'quality time'* in the company of people with whom you can feel at ease and you know that you can be yourself. These people are often described as 'soul-mates', using the term in its widest sense to include friends as well as partners. I often refer to this circle of people as *'family'*.

I hope you noticed the quotation marks around the word 'family'. I use these because nowadays (for better or worse) many people do not obtain the kind of intimacy to which I am referring from blood or even legal relatives. Instead, their 'brothers', 'sisters' and 'mothers and fathers', 'uncles and aunts' and 'children' may be friends or colleagues.

The most important criteria for judging whether someone is suitable for including in your intimacy circle is whether or not there is *mutual caring*, preferably of the unconditional kind, between you. It is difficult to draw much spiritual nurture from people who are always wishing us to be someone we are not! It is also difficult to gain this kind of intimacy from relationships which are *consistently* heavily unbalanced in terms of commitment and caring.

Your intimacy circle or 'family' does not need to know each other, but if a few of them are acquainted and also care for each other, you can gain bonus food from spending time with them as a group. This is why I

> Friend: one who knows all about you and loves you just the same.
> ELBERT HUBBARD

love working so much with personal development groups who meet on a regular basis. It is amazing how the intensely intimate nature of these groups seems to produce even more spiritual food than its members can derive from meeting each other on other occasions. The atmosphere of safety and confidentiality enables people to trust and share openly and freely. But also, very importantly, it also gives people the 'permission' to stay quiet and silent if they choose to do so. (Another good test of the 'intimate' nature of a relationship).

Please understand that I am not saying that relationships which do not fit into this special category of intimacy are not just as worthwhile. It is just that they cannot give us this particular kind of spiritual food so readily. It is better, in my opinion, to face honestly the limits of our personal relationships. I have found many people become frustrated, angry and lonely because they are trying to extract this kind of nurturing from people who cannot or will not give it to them. This is a common and understandable mistake, because we have all been culturally and possibly genetically programmed to expect to obtain intimacy from our relatives, our long-term sexual partners and 'best' friends. When this does not happen, at some level we feel 'cheated' and hurt. A build-up of these kinds of feelings often stops us from taking and appreciating the other positive qualities which the relationship can offer us. So for everyone concerned it is better to face the need for our *spirit* to be fed in this way from other people who are willing and able to give us the kind of intimacy we want.

This means that after a setback we may have to accept that we may not be able to obtain this food from our nearest and dearest, even though we may be drawn towards seeking it from them, and they may feel guilty, inadequate or bad for not being able or willing to give it.

Another important point to remember is that we need to nurture these 'family' relationships if we want them to nurture us in our hours of need. We may need to do this even when we think we cannot afford the time to do so. These relationships must always be very near the top of our priority list. A few years ago I made the quotation shown in the box one of my three most important life rules.

> Spend more time than you think you can afford on the relationships which matter most to you.

I have written this rule down and I repeat it often, so now when I am in a situation where I am trying to make a choice between, for example, doing the housework and spending time with my 'family' there is rarely a contest. Since I made the rule, I have noticed that we still live in a clean-enough house!

Suggestions for Gaining More Intimacy

- Don't rely too heavily on one or two people to give you this food. Always be on the look-out for new 'family'. You don't have to know someone for years and years before they can feed you in this way. Sometimes our oldest friends cannot come up with these 'goods' as easily, for many reasons. A general rule is that we need approximately six 'family' members at any one time. If we have this number, it is likely that at least one will be there for us after a setback.
- Spend more time than you think you can afford on the relationships which matter most to you.
- Disclose as much of your personal thoughts and feelings to your 'family' as you possibly can (while reserving your right to be private sometimes of course.) Self-disclosure (i.e. 'soul-bearing') is the main route to intimacy. If you feel that they will love you less or give you too much hassle for sharing, then find someone else.
- Join a group of people who share common values and talk openly to each other. This does not need to be a 'therapy' group, it could be a group centred around a hobby, as long as it involves free discussion about personal issues and there is genuine caring.
- If for some reason your 'family' has disintegrated (because, for example, children are leaving home, you are going through a divorce, or you have moved house), find a professional person to act as a temporary confidante for a while until you have a new 'family'. This professional person could, for example, be a counsellor, health visitor, aromatherapist or vicar. Loneliness is a good enough reason for asking for this kind of help – you do not have to wait until you have a setback which presents you with an excuse for seeking the kind of intimacy your spirit needs. People who are attracted to this kind of work usually love helping in this way, if they have the time available, and will be flattered if asked. (Remember – it is their responsibility to protect their *own* time and interests, all

you have to do is show respect by asking them if they have the time to talk, or mind that you are sharing in this way.)

– Have imaginary conversations with, or write 'letters' to, someone you have gained intimacy from who is now no longer alive. Very often people I work with will use one of their deceased grandparents for this purpose. I use my friend Britte who died four years ago, but whose 'soul' I can draw upon for intimacy. Once again, remember that you do not have to have religious practice to be able to do this.

Spirit Food 3: Sensory Stimulation

This food is gained from doing activities which arouse one or more of our five senses (sight, hearing, touch, smell and taste). Although obviously it is preferable to experience pleasure rather than pain from this food, the latter is preferable to no sensation at all. Anyone who has been seriously *depressed* (as opposed to just deeply sad) knows how dispiriting it is not to be able to feel some degree of sensory stimulation. Most of us (and, yes, I certainly include myself) would rather feel regular doses of substantial pain rather than be sentenced to a life of feeling 'dead to the world' whatever we are seeing, hearing, touching, smelling or tasting.

Those of you who haven't been depressed may be able to understand what I am saying about the need for sensory stimulation if you think of how you feel when you are bored. Would you rather have an evening being bored by someone or a film than an evening being aroused by a stimulating, fierce argument with a colleague or being aroused to tears by watching a sad play?

Of course, there should be limits to the amount of displeasure to which you should subject yourself. For example, your spirit would not want you to make yourself sick by eating disgustingly foul-tasting spirit food, but it may prefer to try a new slightly over-spiced curry in preference to a totally bland plate of food!

Sensual pleasure is good for the soul!

Suggestions for Finding More Sensory Stimulation

- Look out for, and appreciate, contrasting sensory experiences. The spirit can take extra nurture from, for example: a brilliant blue sky peeping through dark, turbulent clouds, or the gentle sound of a rippling mountain brook after leaving the hustle and bustle of a city, or the taste of a rich sauce against the subtle flavour of new potato or fresh pasta.
- Buy some tapes of naturally stimulating sounds (e.g. the lapping waves or rainforest sounds suggested earlier) as well as some more arousing upbeat music, and take these with your Walkman whenever you are travelling by public transport. (When we are driving ourselves we have to be careful, of course, not to take sounds or music which will relax us too much!)
- Keep a pet and don't forget to stroke and cuddle it!
- Do the same whenever you can with your 'family'!
- If you can't take yourself to stunning scenery in real life, watch it on films or feed on it through illustrated travel books (keep a supply on the coffee table). Alternatively, plaster your walls with scenic photographs and paintings, making sure that you have them in places where you can gaze at them regularly (the loo would do!).
- Treat yourself to warm aromatherapy baths in candlelight instead of showers, at least three times a week.
- Smell and feel your oranges before eating them.
- Make it a rule to buy or borrow some music which is new to you at least once a month.
- Set your alarm to listen to the dawn chorus every so often, and then take a favourite warm drink back to bed with you and snuggle up to ... (or a furry teddy!) until you drift back to sleep again.
- Try one new taste per month (drink or food).
- When going for a walk, touch as well as see. Feel as many different textures as you can.
- Put aromatic oils in the humidifiers on your radiators or in bowls in front of the fire.

– Look for extra stimulation from your senses in ordinary events, for example take a brief moment to appreciate the sparkle on a glass as you polish it dry; the crunching sound as you bite into a crisp apple or the scent and smoothness of freshly laundered sheets.

Spirit Food 4: Passion

This food is related to our last one because it also involves the senses and feelings, but the experiences must be *deeply* moving.

So many people I meet have been starved of this food for many years. This is partly because we draw on its nurturing qualities most when we are almost at the point of losing control. To be able to enjoy this food we need *a high degree of the emotional skills* we discussed in Wheel One. We must be able to feel total confidence in our ability to manage whatever emotion we are experiencing, so that we can trust ourselves not to harm ourselves or anyone else.

Another reason is that many people have become *immunized through the media* against passion. They have perhaps over-dosed on thrilling movies, shocking news and deeply romantic and tear-jerking sagas to have any energy left for them in real life.

A further reason why many people are not receiving as much passion as their spirit needs is that they have become too stressed by *overdose of pressure*. This is, of course, very often the state in which people find themselves after a setback. When we have reached this state, the shutters begin to go down on our emotional systems and however hard we may try to let ourselves 'go' in the arms of someone we know we fancy, or to laugh hilariously at something we know is funny, we find that we cannot. Again this is a very understandable problem, because, in manageable doses, pressure can stimulate our passion, and this is indeed why people may have sought it out in the first place. They may have taken work which was bound to make them feel deeply stirred by emotions such as anger, excitement or compassion, or they may have chosen relationships which stimulated very deep love, or hobbies which arouse panic and fear.

> **Even a tiny dose of Passion can stir your spirit into action.**

After a setback it is easy to forget the positive pull of this food and we may feel inclined to avoid it (e.g. 'I'm never going to let myself fall in love again;' 'I now want an easy, routine, nine-to-five job;' or 'I think I'll stick to knitting and keep away from the bungie jumps in the future.') But let's not forget that you can have too much of *all* our spiritual foods, and passion is no different, *if* we have good-enough emotional skills. So, don't let yourself be afraid of passion after a setback. All you have to do is make sure that you have strengthened Wheel 1 before enjoying these follow-ing suggestions!

Suggestions for Injecting More Passion in Your Life

- Book ahead for nights at passionate *live* theatrical events (e.g. fireworks to rousing music; the opera; giant rock events).
- Do the same for some comedy shows which are guaranteed to make your sides split with laughter, rather than just snigger at the satire.
- Listen to singers with big voices singing from the depths of their souls (Pavarotti, Nina Simone, Elvis ...You could then imagine them singing a song about your setback and see if that helps to lift you).
- Have at least one room in the house coloured with passion. Paint the walls in vibrant colours (you can always smother it in magnolia afterwards if it doesn't work). If it is a lounge or bedroom, scatter it with bright cushions and gaudy knick-knacks and keep some sensual oils burning in it. If you can't set aside one room for stimulating your passion, you can still keep the oils and some brightly coloured throws and exotic paper flowers in a drawer so you can enliven the mood of a normally relaxing room when you feel in need of some extra 'zip' after a setback.

- Allow your wardrobe some room for passion. Next time you go to the sales, make sure that at least a proportion of your 'buys' are wild rather than sensible. We can all afford a few crazy items in our wardrobe. I used to buy my exotic numbers from jumble sales and charity shops when I had very little money.
- Learn a dance which stirs you (and others when they watch you!) – I can recommend the Argentine Tango, and my daughter recommends the Salsa. Our friends in La Puebla de Los Infantes in Spain become instantly uplifted the moment a Flamenco guitarist starts strumming.
- Splash out from time to time on a *luxurious* bunch of flowers or a single stunning rose for someone you care about (this could also be you!).
- If you are invited to a party after a setback and you don't feel like going, set aside an hour before you leave to spend 'revving' yourself up emotionally to be its life and soul (use affirmations, music and thoughts of exciting possibilities, rather than drugs or drink, which are passion-killers the moment they wear off). As an introvert I know this can be hard, but I remind myself that it is possible for every human being to *act* as though they were feeling passionately extrovert for at least a short period of time. I have found that once I have 'forced' myself into that behaviour style, very often the feeling follows.
- Find a cause (unrelated to your current setback) which stirs anger within you and set yourself a short-term action plan to do something for it. You don't have to commit yourself to it for life, just long enough to use your anger to achieve something constructive.

Spirit Food 5: Make-believe

I am writing this at Christmas time while surrounded by a world which is indulging in its craving for this kind of food. Not only are we surrounding ourselves with images of Father Christmas climbing down our non-existent chimneys, we are playing 'let's pretend' games with many real people in our lives. For a short few days, millions among us are putting aside the reality of their stressed, lonely, self-centred lives and living in a make-believe world of close-knit families and communities who are committed to

> Make-believe is a great de-stressor.

caring and sharing and who all have unlimited time and money to spend on fun and food.

I believe that we indulge in the 'madness' of the Christmas spirit not just because we have been commercially 'conned' into doing so, but because it feeds the part of us that needs a dose of make-believe. Those of us who have a tendency to go a good deal 'madder' than is good for our bank balances, livers and relationships, could perhaps try drip-feeding our starved spirits with more regular doses of this food throughout the year, and most especially after we have had a setback.

Suggestions for Make-believing

- Allow yourself regular times to daydream. Set your alarm early once or twice a week and just indulge in some fantasy before facing the reality of today's to-do list.
- Join in children's games either in real life or through watching their programmes on TV.
- Make sure that you have regular doses of fantasy fiction during the week by either reading novels or comics (the latter is one of my esteemed colleague's favourite fantasy antidotes to setback stress!), watching not-so-real-life soaps or films (*my* preferred form of make-believe).
- Throw a fancy dress or theme party.
- Time your holidays to fit in with local festivals and carnivals. Then bury your camera and just join in the fun.
- Start staff meetings with fun fantasy games. (They break the ice, build team-spirit and stimulate creativity if you need to justify the time!)
- Invite magicians and clowns to your conferences instead of, or as well as, motivational speakers.
- Have imaginary consultations with your fairy-godmother whenever you feel stuck in a rut. Imagine her granting

your wish and then see if you can extract a 'grain of possibility' from your fantasy (you may not be able to spend the next week on a desert island away from you-know-who, but perhaps you could treat yourself to some earplugs, a dose of creative visualization and a comforting drink for at least 10 minutes each day).

– Join a drama group – you can feed your spirit even by playing a blade of grass or painting the scenery.

– Organize a staff pantomime – or do a group trip to your local one, dressed in the appropriate 'gear'!

Spirit Food 6: Creation

This food involves creating something new. *Every* toddler I have ever known seems instinctively to want to do this. You show them how to do something and a few minutes later they are inviting you to observe their new way of doing it! You give them a cardboard box and it is immediately transformed into a house or a helmet. You absent-mindedly leave them alone with a box of felt tip pens, and you return to find some colourful 'wall paper'.

By the time these same children reach adulthood, only very few will be labelled by themselves and others as 'creative', and even fewer will actually be doing activities which could be classed as *true* creations. Most will be living highly 'instructed' lives. They will be cooking by recipe, working to guidelines, parenting according to child-care 'bibles', dressing themselves and their homes along the current fashion rules, exercising to fitness routines and singing along to pre-programmed karaoke tunes.

> Setbacks often require us to come up with *new* solutions because the old approaches and methods are no longer working.

I am not disputing the value of these activities – most are very sensible and many are very satisfying. Usually they achieve desired results far more efficiently and speedily than a more experimental approach *might* do. The only danger is that we can rely on them so heavily that we lose faith in our own ability to feed our spirit with creativity. If we have continued to keep our creative juices flowing freely, we are much more likely to be able to respond to these kinds of challenges with fresh, original ideas.

So, if you feel you have left too much of your creativity in the nursery, here are a few suggestions for reviving it now.

Suggestions for Reviving Your Creativity

- Cook one meal per week without the recipe book (either in your kitchen or in your head).
- Make your own Christmas and birthday cards (and feed your spirit even further by sending the money you save to the charity of your choice).
- Start your team meetings occasionally with a creative game (there are now several good books available with ideas, but why not invent your own?!).
- Join an art class or just spend more time doodling.
- Join a drama or creative writing class or group (or go on an activity holiday which provides them).
- Decorate at least one room (or one wall would do) each year in your own original style. If you cannot afford the paint or live in rented rooms, experiment from time to time with moving the furniture around to give it a 'new look'.
- Enrol on an educational course which will encourage you to do some research into an area which has not been studied before.
- When you are standing in a supermarket queue, use the time to look at an object in your trolley and imagine all the different uses it could have (for example, a tin of beans could be a building block; a bookend, a door stop or ...). As soon as the ideas dry up move on to another object, and you will find that you are soon coming up much more quickly with novel ideas.
- Take the newspaper and randomly mark a few stories with a felt tip and then imagine how different they could have been if there had been just one slight change in the circumstances leading up to the event. I heard Colin

Dexter, author of the highly successful *Inspector Morse* TV series, recently say that he usually gets his ideas from asking the question 'What if ...?' – What if it had rained today and we were stuck indoors and ...?; What if that letter had not been a bill but a ransom message for ...?; What if I had married ...?; etc.

– When sitting on public transport, use some time to invent a story around one or more of the passengers. If you are with a friend you can make this into a competitive game (but be discreet in your observations – if you are caught staring you create your own *new* drama!).

> The soul never thinks without a picture.
>
> ARISTOTLE

Spirit Food 7: Personal Growth

This spiritual food is about giving yourself regular opportunities to *learn and develop.*

Setbacks often require that little bit extra from us. Our 'normal' performance level is often not quite good enough because the circumstances of the setback may be *unusually* demanding. *We have to believe that we can extract more from ourselves to match each new challenge.* This belief is likely to weaken if we are in the habit of continually 'coasting' through our everyday lives. Many people I know did not consciously develop this habit, they have just drifted into a pressurized rut. They have given themselves such busy, stressful lives that any learning and self-development project would feel like an extra burden.

> Thrivers are people who are constantly stretching themselves and extending the current limits of their minds and bodies.

But the kind of personal growth that we need to feed our spirit should *never* feel like an encumbrance in our lives. It must either feel like fun or at least spark off a *feeling* of interest and curiosity. Learning which is not like this may be a means to a survivor's end, but it will not feed the soul of a Thriver.

If we feed ourselves with regular doses of *stimulating* personal growth opportunities we will maintain our faith in the elasticity of our potential, without giving ourselves undue pressure. (And remember, there is no danger that we will become overly arrogant or unrealistic because the humility we carry in our Quality Kitbag will remind us that even the strongest elastic has its breaking point!)

Suggestions to Get You Stretching!

- Choose holiday or weekend break destinations or activities which offer you the opportunity to do more than just 'chill out'.
- Occasionally buy a magazine or newspaper which is different from your usual favourite.
- Choose to spend a few of your lunch or coffee breaks with people who you know have different interests or skills to your own, and discover what you can learn from them.
- Browse the Internet for 15 minutes each week with the sole purpose of acquiring some new information on a subject about which you know little (go to an Internet café if you haven't facilities at home).
- Make a New Year's resolution list *twice* a year (use your birthday or your summer holiday as a marking point) and include a new personal growth challenge in each (e.g. learning a new skill or hobby, altering a behaviour, developing a new habit, etc.). If you are stuck for ideas, ask a confrontative, honest friend for ideas on how you could improve yourself!
- Join a personal development group with a leader who practises what they preach (i.e. they have a history of having stretched their own potential).
- Keep some self-improvement books and cassettes in *accessible* places (e.g. on your bedside table, on your desk or beside the bath). Make a habit of dipping into them from time to time even when you are not aware of being in need of inspiration and motivation. If their 'advice' or style appears to have lost its 'bite' (sounds too much like

common sense), visit the bookshop or library immediately and find a new, more challenging one. Don't wait for the next setback to prompt you into self-improvement reading and activity.

Spirit Food 8: Communal Action

This spiritual food is the one that satisfies our social needs. Setbacks can sometimes leave us feeling very lonely and iso-lated even if the reality is that we are not. This is particularly true of natural introverts like myself. As soon as we meet a problem, we have a tendency to pull down our shutters on the world and run into a corner to 'hibernate' until the crisis has passed or we have found a solution on our own.

These difficult times are when we may need to feel sup-ported not just by our close 'family', but also by a much wider community who share our basic values and interests. If, for example, I am robbed by a mugger, I need the immediate comfort which my own 'family' can provide, but it also helps me to know that I am part of a local community which would angrily leap to my defence if they were to witness such an abuse taking place, and also a member of a national or inter-national society which has laws against this abuse of my human rights.

I can only draw meaningful sustenance from such support, however, if my own personal spirit is strongly connected to these larger 'spiritual forces' outside my immediate 'family' world.

The bigger our political, economic and social communities become, the more *conscious concerted effort* we may need to make to ensure that we have this kind of connection with our community. There are many, many advantages in the modern trend towards globalization of our communities, but one of its disadvantages is that it makes this kind of spiritual food much harder to acquire. This is partly because it is obtained by join-ing together with others (in spite of differences) in forms of *communal activity* which reinforce our shared spirit. The larger the community, the harder it is to organize activities which involve all its members in a meaningful way. But it is also partly because we do not have infallible human natures, and the larger the group the more likely we are to sit back and expect others to provide for this need.

> Thrivers make sure they are connected to the community around them!

Suggestions for Communal Action

- Make the time to take part in more community rituals, such as local carnivals, fêtes and parades, New Year celebrations outside the home, and group carol singing.
- Have more 'family' feasts. As more and more of us are working 'unsocial hours', eating fast food or special diets, it is becoming harder to maintain the tradition of family feasting which is still an instinctive as well as a traditional way of bonding a group of people together. Our own family evolved its own informal rules to ensure this spiritual need was met to at least some degree even when we were all at our busiest and most independent stages of our lives. When we are living in the same house, we all make it a top priority to have a very lengthy Sunday breakfast and a late evening cup of tea and snack together.
- Make social events for your work team a regular occurrence and not an annual event, *and* ensure that they are affordable and open to all.
- Make the company you work for, or own, take more responsibility for attending and financially supporting community events.
- Go to football matches or TV screenings in public places instead of watching them at home.
- Attend or participate in national and international Arts Festivals, especially those which have live performances.
- Attend funeral and memorial services of people whom you may not have known very well, but whose lives had some meaning for you or your community. I am sure *one* of the reasons why so many people converged on London after Princess Diana's death was because *they* needed more community.

- Attend public demonstrations of causes which you support.
- Join or start community or residents' action groups.
- Make time to go out of your way to sign or start petitions.
- Canvas, either formally or informally, for community policies in which you believe, through starting political debates at election time!
- Join (rather than just donate to) national or international action organizations.

A human being is part of the whole, called by us 'Universe'; a part limited in time and space. He experiences himself, his thoughts, and feelings as something separated from the rest - a kind of optical delusion of his consequence. Our task must be to free ourselves from this prison by widening our circle of compassion to embrace all living creatures, and the whole of nature in its beauty.

ALBERT EINSTEIN

Spirit Food 9: Servitude

I am I plus my surroundings and if I do not preserve the latter, I do not preserve myself.

JOSÉ ORTEGA Y GASSET

Every morning, whatever the time and whatever the weather, when I take my dog for a walk I see various individuals stop by the lakeside, on their way to work, to feed the swans. Most of these people are on their own and they arrive by all manner of transport. Among the more ordinary cars and bikes which arrive, there is a bus, a refuse lorry, a taxi, and a couple of impressive limousines. These people do not come to walk, talk or be seen, they come merely to feed the birds. Once their job is done, they depart. They receive no thanks or admiration from either the birds or those of us in the world who take so much pleasure from the beauty and serenity this wildlife brings to our community.

I have never spoken to any of these individuals, so I cannot tell you if they are saints or sinners, and I can only guess at the 'reasoning' behind their selfless commitment. *It makes them feel good.* And I would hazard a further guess that it makes them feel good because they are not just feeding the swans at the start to every day, they are feeding their spirit.

To obtain this food we must engage in activities which help others in need, or just help the world in general to become a better and more enduring and beautiful place.

> Everybody can be great ... because anybody can serve. You don't have to have a college degree to serve ... you only need a heart full of grace.
>
> MARTIN LUTHER KING

Of course it is not *easy* for any of us to be genuinely altruistic or generous, but it is especially hard when we live in a society which is continually panicking about the limits of its resources and which is also highly cynical and suspicious of anyone who has the slightest shadow of a halo. But our spirits do appreciate good effort! And (although perhaps it is not very saintly of me to say this) you may eventually reap a reward for your efforts at your next setback. Commonly, these turn out to be 'pay-back' times. It is often not until we reach a crisis that we are confronted with the wisdom in the saying *'As you sow, so shall you reap.'*

So, if you feel that your spirit could benefit from a slightly increased dose of servitude, here are a *few* suggestions. There are not many because I am sure you are as aware as I am of what you *could* do but don't do!

Suggestions for Servitude

- Feed the swans in your community! You can do this either literally or metaphorically (i.e. do anything which will help your local community to become a more pleasant and beautiful place).
- Make it a rule to do at least one good deed a day, and keep a check on yourself by developing a habit of remembering

> Servitude in its purest form is selfless activity without the need or hope of reward or admiration.

that deed as you brush your teeth before going to bed. If you have let yourself down, simply plan two good works for the next day.

– Give an anonymous donation to a charity.
– Scatter some wildflower seeds on a barren-looking hedgerow.
– Every six months take the clothes you haven't worn to a charity shop (*and* feed your soul even further by washing and ironing them first).
– Walk, cycle or travel by public transport whenever you can.
– Recycle and repair even when you do not need to save the money.
– Donate time or money to an ecology project.

> A great ocean creates a great soul in people, and the diminishment of the ocean diminishes the people.
> THOMAS MOORE, AUTHOR OF *CARE OF THE SOUL*

Spirit Food 10: Appreciation

You'll be pleased to know that your spirit should already have had an injection of this kind of nourishment. (I am assuming, of course, that you've already worked diligently through my previous section on how to top up your Humility – pages 19–22!)

This food is obtained by setting time aside to show respect, admiration and gratitude for 'The Great and the Good' around us. Like most of our spiritual foods, traditionally most people have found it through the practice of their religion. Participating in services or rituals which are designed to pay respects to gods and saints is probably still the most common and well-known source of appreciation. (In its religious form it is often called 'veneration'.) This is why they are sometimes attended even by people who have 'lost' their faith. But increasingly many people, even those who maintain a belief in an Almighty power, are seeking something different to this kind of practice. They are finding this spiritual food through other forms of activity. I have already mentioned a number of these in my list of tips on humility. And I am sure you know many more yourself. But in case your memory needs a jog in the right direction, here are a few suggestions on how you can obtain Appreciation through secular means.

Suggestions for Appreciation

- Visiting the wonders of the man-made world and encouraging others to do so.
- Visiting nature's spectacular achievements and supporting their upkeep with donations.
- Attending live performances of high achievers in the worlds of music and sport, and clapping, stamping or singing to express your appreciation.
- Listening to lectures and talks given by great thinkers, teachers and innovators, and then personally thanking them for their inspiration.
- Writing fan mail (or even a poem) to 'gurus'.
- Writing letters of thanks to people who have achieved wonders, if only in your eyes.
- Buying biographies of great men and women and reading them (ostentatiously!) on trains and planes and then passing them on to friends.
- Autograph hunting.
- Erecting statues and portraits in public places or in our offices and homes.
- Placing flowers on the graves of, or special places associated with, people we have admired and are no longer living.
- Writing in Visitors' books to express our esteem of the people and place we have been to visit.
- Composing, playing or listening to significant music in appreciation.
- Awarding medals, certificates, stars or prizes for others' outstanding achievement and effort.
- Frequently giving carefully chosen presents as tokens of respect and not just in response to annual rituals.

> Appreciation feeds the soul of its giver as well as that of its receiver.

Instant Exercise

Skim-read this chapter again and write down *one* aspect of fitness to which you will give *priority* attention during the next month.

Physical _____

Mind _____

Spiritual _____

> A worldly loss often turns into spiritual gain.
>
> HAZRAT INAYAT KHAN

HELEN KELLER 1880–1968

At 19 months, Helen developed an illness which rendered her blind and deaf. Her life was a continual struggle to cope with the 'stillness and darkness' which enveloped her. Through her own incredible persistence and courage and the help of dedicated teachers, she learned to communicate through Braille and sign language. She went on to gain an honours degree and become an inspiring lecturer, writer, political activist and fund-raiser for the blind and deaf.

CHAPTER 4

Planning
Your
Route

You are now ready to set off on your journey – or are you?

You are a Thriver and now sitting on some excellent wheels. You have the qualities, skills and strength to meet any manner of challenge. But are you sure you know where you want to go in life, and what kind of ride you want to give yourself to get there?

It is possible that you are someone who thinks that these are not your choices. You may believe that these are decisions made by a higher power, the stars or the random hand of fate. But if you believe that there is a grain of truth in that well-known saying *'Life is what you make it'*, then read on – we are now going to do some route planning. You will be looking at the kind of:

1   Destination you are hoping to arrive at (i.e. your life dream).
2   Terrain you want your journey to take you through (i.e. your preferred lifestyle).
3   Problems and dangers you may meet (i.e. potential setbacks).

4   Contents of your SOS breakdown kit (i.e. your plans for emergency self-care).

I cannot guarantee, of course, that by doing this planning work you will achieve success. But I do believe that *you will be increasing the odds in favour of arriving at your chosen destination and will be cycling along the kind of path you will enjoy.* One of the main reasons behind my belief is that I have observed that most people's *confidence* is greatly enhanced by life planning, and I know that when we are confident we undoubtedly have a much easier path through life and are more likely to achieve our goals and recover from any kind of setback.

But of course planning and confidence cannot protect us entirely. I have had many both serious and not-so-serious setbacks in my life which I could never have avoided even with the most careful of life-plans. But what I have now learned is how to recover more efficiently and remotivate myself with a new or modified plan. I know that this proactive approach has brought me much more happiness and satisfaction while journeying to whatever destination I eventually reach than my earlier cynical *'what will be, will be'* philosophy ever did.

> Pain nourishes courage. You can't be brave if you have only had wonderful things happen to you.
>
> MARY TYLER MOORE

Instant Workout – My Destination

1   Select a date in the *long-distance future* which you wish to work towards (10/15/25 years' hence).
2   Choose six adjectives to describe how you would like to *feel* at that time (confident/at peace, etc.).
3   Choose six adjectives to describe the kind of *lifestyle* you would want to be leading (varied/peaceful/challenging, etc.).
4   Briefly describe the kind of *home and community* you would like to be living in.

5   Which *people in your current life* would you most like to
    have sharing your life with you (limit yourself to 10!).
6   Use six adjectives to describe the qualities you would be
    looking for *in people whom you would like* to be in your life
    at that point.
7   Briefly describe the work (paid or unpaid) you would like
    to be engaged in doing.
8   List the three main hobbies/social pastimes you would
    like to have.
9   List three new skills you
    would like to have
    acquired (personal/work-
    related or social).
10 List the six key adjectives
    you would like people to
    be using to describe you
    by that time.

> People forget so easily what it is they want. They go one step down the road to try to get it, and then get caught up in the way they are trying. They don't notice that the *way* they have chosen doesn't work.
>
> RICHARD BANDLER

Instant Workout – My Route

Using our cycling metaphor, which kind of road would you
prefer to take to reach your destination?

1   Easy, quick, straight motorway route through flat
    countryside.
2   Winding road through rolling country and the occasional
    congested village and town.
3   Mountainous route with spectacular scenery, but
    unpredictable weather and potentially dangerous terrain.

POTENTIAL SETBACKS

List six potential setbacks which, with your current knowledge, you anticipate you could meet on your chosen route.

1   People who might let you down (in the light of any
    weaknesses they may have already shown).

2 Shortfall in external resources (in the light of your past experience and the size of the risks you might have to take).

3 Health problems (in the light of any current weakness you know you currently have).

4 Mistakes you could make (in the light of your current knowledge about yourself, your past and potential).

5 Other...

6 Other...

Instant Workout – My SOS Kit

Knowing the kind of journey you have chosen and the setbacks which you may meet, complete the following lists to put into your Kitbag (with your mobile phone of course!) as reminders of what you could do if you meet a setback.

1 Names of people I could depend on to give me:

practical support _____

emotional sustenance _____

professional advice _____

financial advice or loan _____

other _____

2 Quick treats you could give to rebuild your self-esteem:

_____

_____

_____

3   List three quick mood-changing exercises you could use to
     stop you becoming depressed (see Chapter 8 for some
     ideas or choose your own).

_____

_____

_____

One of the first things that a young person must internalize, deep down in the blood
and bones, is the understanding that although he may en route have many defeats, he
must not be defeated. If life teaches you anything, it may be that it is necessary to
suffer some defeats.

                                                                      MAYA ANGELOU

PABLO NERUDA 1904–1973

The Chilean poet Pablo Neruda's mother died within a
month of his birth. He was a shy and lonely child who began
writing poetry at 10 years old. He was so discouraged by his
father that when he began publishing he did so under a pseu-
donym, which he was later to adopt legally as his own name.
He spent much of his early adulthood in extreme poverty and
his subsequent career was peppered with continual ups and
downs. He courageously used his poetry to highlight social
and political injustices, and became known as the poet of
'enslaved humanity'. He spent long periods in exile from
Chile, but was eventually able to return rich and famous, and
even became its ambassador to France. He received the Nobel
prize for literature and is generally recognized as the most
important Latin American poet of the 20th century.

CHAPTER 5

Recovering from Minor Setbacks

> Success is relative:
>   It is what we can make of the mess
> we have made of things.
>
> T. S. ELIOT

What is a *minor* setback? You tell me!

Seriously, what seems minor to you may seem major to me and vice versa. And what you may see as minor today may become major tomorrow. And what seems major today may look very minor by tomorrow.

So in the light of these incontestable truths, I am reluctant to list examples. But I must, in order to clarify my own meaning, make it easier for you to understand where and how to apply the material in this chapter. In writing it I had in mind the following kind of 'everyday' setbacks:

- failing your expectations in an exam
- being turned down for a job or course
- having a no-win argument with a friend or colleague (as opposed to having one with a member of your 'family' or a boss)

- cancellation of a holiday due to poor weather or mismanagement
- a too-late arrival of something such as: a part needed for a repair, a long-awaited report (or, indeed, a manuscript for a book!)
- a breakdown which causes your late arrival at the airport and causes you to miss your flight
- a dose of flu or measles which stops you from doing an important presentation
- being turned down by an attractive person for a date
- decorating a room in a colour or wallpaper which looks hideous once the deed is done
- buying an expensive item of clothing for an important event and finding out the night before that it doesn't fit or clashes with your jacket
- losing a contract or failing with an important project because you were the wrong person for the job
- dropping the meal you made for a celebration dinner as you take it out of the oven.

I hope you get the picture, and I don't need to raid my personal museum of setbacks for examples any longer. (It's tasks like this that make me momentarily wonder if I am cycling down the right road!)

However 'little' such experiences may seem in the light of the greater hindrances and obstacles I have met, I know that at the time, they can feel like impassable road blocks. Indeed they can *become* impassable road blocks. I know, because for many years I allowed this to happen. I would become so irritated or despairing that I would give up on whatever it was that I was trying to do.

Later, I would sometimes look back and feel ashamed at my lack of courage or persistence, but at other times I would look back with bitterness and curse the hand of fate or even life itself for being so unfair. Needless to say neither reaction would inspire me to try again. If I thought I was a loser, the world around me thought I was a loser, and I therefore became a loser. If I thought I was a victim, I started to behave like one and would allow others to shower even more setbacks in my way. And then of course, when the big setbacks came I had no hope of winning.

My turnaround was undoubtedly precipitated by the *major* disasters in my early adult life, but it was the subsequent mini ones which I have to thank for the building of the new strength which has helped me cope with the more recent major ones. Without the practice at making success from these minor setbacks, I am convinced I would not be writing this book today.

When I sat down to reflect on what I, and others, had started to do that had made the difference, as usual a pattern began to emerge. From this pattern I have designed the following strategy which I hope you will find a useful step-by-step guide. It can be applied to most setbacks whether or not they are caused by our own mistakes or failings or by those of others, or fate or a mixture of both. I hope my examples will illustrate how this can be done.

The reminder mnemonic sentence is:

Creating Success From Little Setbacks Builds Morale

The first letter of each of the words in the sentence is also the first letter of each of the key steps:

Calm
Self-esteem
Facts
Learning
Strategy
Back-up
Motivation

Now let's look at each in turn.

Step 1: Calm

The first task is to take control of our anxiety, fear, anger, disappointment or guilt. If we want to make a success out of the situation, we need to ensure

> When we are unable to find tranquillity within ourselves, it is useless to seek it elsewhere.
> FRANÇOIS LA ROCHEFOUCAULD

that we, and not our emotions, are in control. It is unwise to look at or work on a solution in the outside world until we are in a state of tranquillity, because, as we have noted several times before, our thinking brain cannot function at its most efficient until we are in this *physiological* state.

We need to do this even if our feelings are totally justified, are even a 'sane' or 'human' response to what has happened. But it is of course especially true if the emotion we are feeling is disproportionate or not appropriate to the situation. It may take different action to induce a state of calm, but nevertheless the reason for doing so and outcome should be the same.

HOW TO FIND THE CALM WITHIN YOURSELF

> No matter what happens don't panic. The panic stricken individual cannot think or act effectively.
> JOHN PAUL GETTY

- Stop doing whatever you are doing.
- Take yourself to a peaceful location (if you can).
- Unlock any locked or folded limbs.
- Uncurl your fingers and toes.
- Support your body – put both feet on the floor if standing, place your lower back against the chair if sitting, lie down flat if you have the space and opportunity.
- Take three or four deep breaths, following each breath as it goes in and out.
- Check the level of tension in your limbs.
- Do tension-release exercises as necessary.
- Take three more deep breaths.
- Re-check your physical state. If you need more calm do another exercise of your choice such as meditation, a visualization or affirmations (see page 152).

- Safely express bottled-up emotion if you are still not calm (cry if the tears are bursting to get through; throw a cushion if you need to let some anger out – see page 154).
- Repeat the calming exercises for as long as you need to.

Step 2: Self-esteem

> Failure: Is it a limitation? Bad timing? It's a list of things. It's something you can't be afraid of, because you'll stop growing. The next step beyond failure could be your biggest success in life.
>
> DEBBIE ALLEN

This is obviously a more crucial step if the fault behind the setback is yours and yours alone. But even if the blame is fairly and squarely on the shoulders of someone else, it can only do you some good to work through this step. Thrivers cannot have too much self-esteem, especially if they are riding in the fast lane of life. So take a dose·of one or more of the following quick fixes until you have completely restored your faith in yourself and your ability to succeed in spite of the setback.

- Remind yourself of your strengths; list six on a card and put it by your bed or on the bathroom mirror for the next few days. Read the list aloud at least once a day.
- Spend time with a friend or 'family' member who thinks you're great – even if this is only 5 minutes on the phone, talking about the weather.
- Take the dog for a walk, give the cat a cuddle, feed your fish or take some bread to the ducks in the park.
- Comb or re-arrange your hair, spray yourself with your favourite fragrance and give yourself a smile in the mirror.
- Give yourself a food or drink treat, but make sure that it doesn't have a sting in the tail (i.e. is fattening when you think you are too fat already, or will make you drunk and do or say things which will decrease your self-esteem).
- Take a look at last month's or year's diary and remind yourself of at least one success. Close your eyes for a minute and recall the feeling.
- Spend time doing a task which you enjoy and you are especially good at doing, even if it seems quite ordinary to you, but others may appreciate (baking scones, or being nice to difficult customers).
- Do a good turn for someone in need.
- Give a donation to a charity.
- Let some genuinely caring person give you some physical TLC (Tender Loving Care!). An aromatherapy massage from a therapist who talks non-stop about *her* holiday plans for next year does not count!
- Take an appropriate affordable dose of 'retail therapy' (e.g. a *small* extravagance for a minor setback).
- Write a card or e-mail to a friend to whom you have been meaning to write for ages.
- Buy yourself a bunch of flowers or a plant.
- Think what your favourite comedian might say to cheer you up if he or she knew about this setback?
- Talk to a friend who will help you see the funny side of the situation or give you a gentle amusing tease to ease its sting (*not* a hurtful put-down).

> Do not think of your faults; still less of others' faults; look for what is good and strong; and try to imitate it. Your faults will drop off, like dead leaves, when their time comes.
>
> JOHN RUSKIN

If none of the above works, get hold of a copy of my book or cassette entitled *Self Esteem*, and give yourself a more thorough psychological overhaul (who doesn't need this from time to time?!).

MARLEE MATLIN

Marlee became deaf at the age of 2 and had the added burden of having a father who suffered with alcoholism. As a young adult she was tormented by feelings of insecurity and self-doubt, made worse by many failed attempts to settle in jobs in the hearing world. She was continually frustrated by not being able to express her personality. Eventually she found a way to do so through an acting career. She became an international star playing the part of a hearing- and speech-disabled woman in the 1986 film *Children of a Lesser God*.

Step 3: Facts

Now you are in a better state of mind, I hope to help you face the facts. The questions below are the kind you may need to ask yourself. Please note that you are looking at the facts and not the reason behind them for the moment. We will be looking at that later. By looking at the facts first you will have to activate the adult, logical side of you. When you then move on to looking at the 'whys' of the setback, you should do so from a more rational stance and will be less likely to get stuck in the unhelpful 'poor me' or 'wicked me' modes.

If you have time, write your answers to the following questions which are appropriate to your setback. You can then edit out the unnecessary superlative adjectives and adverbs which may be keeping you in a negative frame of mind (e.g. *I chose some [dreadful] wallpaper which makes the room look dark; that [ungrateful, insensitive, lazy] .... let me down again).*

It may help to do this task with another person, but be careful to choose someone who can be objective (not, for example, your partner if he or she is not very pleased about your mistake, or the colleague who caused you the problem).

INSTANT WORKOUT – ANALYSING THE FACTS OF A SETBACK

Think of a minor setback which you have had recently, and try answering the following questions.

- What actually happened? Rather than 'catastrophizing' on what nearly happened or could have happened – areas on which you do not necessarily need to dwell (but I used to do so regularly), think about what really did happen.
- Has this happened before?
- What is the cost of what happened in terms of money, time, materials or other resources?
- Has damage been done to my psychological or emotional or physical health which may need attention?
- How many people have been, or could be, affected by this setback? (Name names or give exact numbers if you can.)
- Have any relationships been damaged? If so, can they be repaired? Do I want to repair them?!
- On a scale of 1–10, what disaster rating would I give this setback? (Rate it 10 only if it is going to kill you.)
- What, in percentage terms, are the chances of this setback happening again?

> Do not weep. Do not wax indignant. Understand.
>
> BARUCH SPINOZA

NORMAN CROUCHER 1941–

At the age of 19, Norman lost both his legs in a railway accident. In his determination to fight back, he walked the length of England on his new metal legs. After many setbacks he became a mountaineer and climbed Mont Blanc. He has worked throughout his career to promote sports for the disabled. He was the first physically handicapped person to be appointed a member of the Sports Council in England.

Step 4: Learning

> Failure is, in a sense, the highway to success, in as much as every discovery of what is false leads us to seek earnestly after what is true.
>
> JOHN KEATS

This is probably the most important key to making success out of your setback in the strategy. When I first realized the positive power of identifying the learning from the setback, I developed a tendency to skip the first three steps of this strategy. What was even worse was that I tried to force my children to do so as well. Fortunately I had also trained them to be assertive, and they would inform me when I did so!

We are much more inclined to do this stage effectively if our self-esteem has been repaired and we are in the adult, thinking part of our personality and not still in our 'child' mindset.

Depending on the nature of your setback, you will need to ask yourself one or more of these questions. Remember that there is always something we can learn from every setback, even if we have learned the lesson before and forgotten it!

> Sell your cleverness and buy bewilderment.
>
> JALAL-UDDIN RUMI

WHAT HAVE I LEARNED FROM THIS SETBACK:

- about my current level of skills and/or knowledge?
- that I need to change about my behaviour?
- about my values and priorities?
- about my potential?
- about the people involved?
- about the kind of support I need?
- about the resources I currently have available?
- that is likely to work well?
- that is unlikely to be achievable either now or ever?
- about the positive aspects of the setback?

> Whatever I have learned I am in the process of learning. What has worked for me this afternoon may not work for me this evening.
>
> MAYA ANGELOU

Step 5: Strategy

Now it is time to make an action plan. How elaborate this needs to be will depend, of course, on the nature of your setback. Remember you might need two action plans.

> Life can only be understood backwards; but it must be lived forwards.
>
> SØREN KIRKEGAARD

1 One for taking action to *right the wrong* of your setback (e.g. a study plan for the re-sit of the exam, or finding another member of staff, or redecorating the room).
2 The second might concern your *personal development needs* (e.g. change a behaviour; re-evaluate your priorities; practise your emotional skills).

> Knowing is not enough; we must act. Willing is not enough; we must do.
>
> JOHANN WOLFGANG VON GOETHE

Find some paper and a pen (remember that we know that goals and plans set down in writing are much more likely to meet with success) and write down what you are going to do (or what you could have ideally done) to make a success out of a recent minor setback.

- If one goal is sufficient, use the *Aim for the Stars* goal-setting strategy on pages 169–171.

- If you need to include both long- and short-term goals, write out your action plan using the *Good Strategies Reap Success* guidelines on page 165.

> Today's opportunities erase yesterday's failures.
>
> GENE BROWN

Step 6: Back-up

Having learned what you now know from experiencing your setback, you have of course greatly increased your chances of being successful with your next effort. But, as you know, there can be no guarantees in this kind of work. Even if you do your part, you may not be able to control others or the environment, or the stock exchange, or the weather. So it is always wise to also prepare a Contingency Plan. This will help to give you courage because you know that you can cope with failure should you have to meet it again. So don't put away your pen and paper just yet. Answer the following questions first.

What could go wrong?

How will I be able to spot this happening at an early stage?

What would be my first action if I was unable to stop it happening? (e.g. start the first steps of *Creating Success From Little Setbacks Builds Morale* strategy again!)

To whom could I turn for the best support in this situation?

Step 7: Motivation

This step is particularly important if you are going to try again to do what may have failed last time. But even if you are excited about doing something new, it's wise not to take your level of motivation for granted.

> Even eagles need a push.
>
> DAVID McNALLY

> All we need to make us really happy is something to be enthusiastic about.
>
> CHARLES KINGSLEY

INSTANT WORKOUT: INCREASING MY MOTIVATION

In relation to the setback you were working on, ask yourself the following questions:

- What am I going to gain if I am successful?
- What would others be likely to gain?
- What treats could I give myself to inspire me on the way?
- Which affirmations could I use to keep me positive?
- Which of my favourite quotes could I use to inspire me? (You might be able to take one or two from this book!)
- Which hero or heroine could I bring to mind if I need a morale booster? (Again, why not choose one of the examples in this book, unless someone else has leapt into your mind?)
- What could I give myself as a final reward?
- To whom could I show my goals or action plan and ask them to give me a nudge from time to time to make sure I stay on track?
- Where could I put my goals or action plans so that I don't forget them?

> There are no birds in last year's nest.
>
> PROVERB

> If the sky falls we shall catch larks!
> PROVERB
>
> Wonders will never cease!
> PROVERB

NICOLA HORLICK 1961–

Nicola was born in England. Her grandparents were Jewish Polish refugees. At the start of her meteoric rise in the male world of City finance, she experienced a personal setback when her 2-year-old daughter was diagnosed with leukaemia. Nicola battled through the practical consequences of this life-threatening diagnosis, which brought setback after setback. When approximately 10 years later she was unfairly suspended from a high-flying post, she fought to be reinstated. Although she did not return to this job, through her skilled use of the media attention her case had gained she became a national heroine. She has used her fame to publicize the issues of working women and wrote a book on her experience to raise funds for her daughter's hospital. Her daughter recently died and Nicola continues to use her personal tragedy to help other children and women.

CHAPTER 6

The Five-Star Treatment Programme for Major Setbacks

I hope you never have to *use* this chapter. Conversely, I also hope you will decide to read it even if you are currently riding along an apparently endless, smooth path to your desired destination.

Some people lead such consistently charmed lives that they would never know how it feels to have their progress turned upside-down by a major setback. Others may have become so skilled at making a success out of minor setbacks that they are able to take a major knock well in their stride. But I am assuming that at least some of you will meet such a severe block or such a long series of minor blows, that you may need (and deserve) more intensive recovery 'treatment' than we have previously looked at.

In the last 25 years of my life, I have needed this kind of five-star programme on at least 12 occasions. Even with all the

> Before my accident I thought a hero was someone who commits a courageous action without considering the consequences.
>
> Now I think a hero is an ordinary individual who finds the strength to persevere and endure in spite of overwhelming obstacles.
>
> CHRISTOPHER REEVE

wisdom I have now acquired on the subject, I doubt that I could ever have predicted most of these setbacks. So I hope you will read on just in case yours or anyone else's luck should turn, and you may need to use the support of this ready-made strategy to help you through.

What is a *major* setback?

I would suggest that it is *any unwelcome block which has such a severe effect on your lifestyle, health, welfare or work that you are unable to continue your normal everyday life for a substantial period of time, or even permanently.*

The kinds of block which can cause this kind of disruption are:

- redundancy
- severe physical or mental health illness or disablement
- divorce/separation
- enforced re-location
- failure of crucial set of exams
- substantial burglary
- rape or other severe sexual trauma
- the 'emptying of the nest'
- death of a loved one
- making a mistake (such as a driving error) leading to severe injury of others
- criminal conviction of self or 'family'
- major financial crisis
- loss through a natural disaster such as a flood, hurricane or earthquake
- major accident.

The impact of any of these will differ from person to person, depending on, for example, our relative:

- health
- psychological strength
- social and personal coping skills
- support
- economic situation

- degree of emotional commitment to whatever has been lost or damaged.

Many of these factors are hidden from the outside world, so it is often difficult for observers to understand why some people crumble and others stand surprisingly upright under the strain. Sometimes our own response can even be a shock to ourselves, because we may not have been aware of the current strength of one or more of these factors. In our surprise it is easy to divert our attention to trying to understand the response to the setback. If this happens, we need to remind ourselves, or anyone else who has started to drift into 'amateur psychologist' mode, that effective treatment and recovery are our top priorities.

So let's proceed to looking at what this means in terms of our psychological recovery and treatment which, needless to say, is just as important as any other action you may need to take.

If we have been seriously physically injured, few people would argue that we should try to obtain the very best available and affordable treatment as soon as possible. I have therefore used the kind of treatment programme you might have for an injury to your body as a metaphor for this strategy. For once, I am not asking you to remember a mnemonic, but merely to recall the following five main stages you might go through after receiving a severe physical injury:

1 Casualty
2 Intensive care
3 Treatment
4 Rehabilitation
5 Convalescence

> A major crisis is neither the best nor most appropriate time to reflect on, or make judgements about, our own or anyone else's ability to cope or survive. We can (and should) look with hindsight at possible preventative measures for the future when these tasks have been completed.

Now let's see in detail how the same stages can be applied to caring for our psychological needs.

Casualty Treatment

RESUSCITATION BY SKILLED DOCTORS OR PARAMEDICS

You could be in an hysterical state and quite unable to make decisions for yourself. You may need to allow yourself to be temporarily guided by experienced, trained professionals or competent volunteers or friends until your mind has recovered some tranquillity and you can think clearly for yourself.

Our thinking brain cannot work effectively when we are in a state of high emotional arousal, even though we may be convinced that we are sure we know the answers. It is likely that it is the Child within us that has found the solution, and therefore it may be an immature or out-of-date response.

But, it is crucial for our psychological health that we can *trust* whoever is taking care of our decision-making at this time.

I clearly remember that a few weeks before my daughter died, I met an undertaker at a party. I talked to him about his work and was so impressed with his caring and committed approach to his work that I made a mental note that I would have complete faith in this man if ever I was unlucky enough to need this kind of professional service. I cannot place too high a value on the role this man and his professional skill and staff played in the immediate aftermath of my daughter's accident. The extra pressure of making the decisions which he made so competently on my behalf may have been just one unbearable straw too many.

This experience has taught me (or re-taught me, perhaps I should say!) the importance of finding this kind of help *before* the setback has occurred. I was lucky (or guided, if you believe in coincidence theories), but I know not everyone is so fortunate. Many people I counsel have become dangerously distraught simply because they haven't known whom to turn to for emergency help.

Instant Exercise – My Emergency 'Staff'

Do you have on file the names and telephone numbers of these kinds of reputable and caring professionals or helpers should you meet an emergency? It's always advisable to have at least two options.

- solicitor
- doctor
- social worker
- mental health advisor or counsellor
- financial advisor
- child carer
- carer for your pets
- undertaker
- other ...

Are these people's details in an accessible place where others may be able to find them if you are unable to do so?

> A clay pot sitting in the sun will always be a clay pot. It has to go through the white heat of the furnace to become porcelain.
>
> MILDRED WITTE STOUVEN

EMERGENCY SURGERY

Do you need to have your contact with anyone 'put in quarantine' so you can recover in peace? I found this to be so in many severe setback situations. You may need to ensure that you are protected at least temporarily from contact with, for example:

- an ex-partner
- a member of your 'family' who is too needy or controlling
- a busy-body in the neighbourhood or at work
- creditors
- the media
- aggressive customers
- any negative thinker!

How would you arrange for this to happen? Would you need an answer-phone, a hide-away or even a bodyguard? Whom could you depend on to ensure your protection?

A RECUPERATIVE CUP OF OVER-SUGARED TEA

During a major setback, we cannot always get our comfort from an *ideal* carer. I have found that it is important to soak up *whatever comfort is on offer* even if it comes in a form which you would normally find unhelpful or distasteful. Remember in this situation you are a 'beggar'– you can be a 'chooser' later!

So, as the Transactional Analysis theorists might say, lock up the Critical Parent in you and let the Adapted Child in you enjoy being comforted by anyone playing Nurturing Parent who wants to indulge! (See my book *Super Confidence* for a summary of this very useful theory of the personality.)

A BLOOD TRANSFUSION

If you have been pre-programmed like me to plunge into deep depression as soon as a major setback arrives, make sure that you can count on an injection of no-nonsense positive thinking. You may even need a daily boost for a while.

Ideally, you need a highly optimistic and assertive person who will repeatedly feed *positive messages over and over again into your subconscious mind, either* in words *or* through their actions. Your job is merely to suppress your inclination to prove them wrong! The kind of messages you need to hear at this stage are along these lines:

> We *will* get through this.
> No, there may not be an obvious answer, but we *will* find one.
> We *will* overcome this.
> There *will* be a solution, even if we do not yet have the answer.
> You *will* recover, however long it may take.

If you haven't this kind of person available, plaster your room with posters with these messages on. Alternatively, record a tape for yourself or buy a positive-thinking tape and play it on a Walkman over and over again.

STITCHES, PLASTER OR TIGHT BANDAGING

You may need some temporary quick-fixes to hold you or your life ticking over until you are healed. You are in survival mode for the moment – you can start Thriving later! You may have to take action, or allow others to do so which you might disapprove of in normal circumstances – for example:

- eating forbidden foods
- letting the children stay up late
- skipping the mortgage payment for one month
- taking a loan from a parent or best friend or the pawnbroker
- delegating an important task to someone less efficient than yourself
- pulling a few strings
- taking a sleeping tablet
- taking anti-depressant medication.

AUTHORITATIVE NURSING TO KEEP YOU IN HOSPITAL

Once again your bossy friend might have a role. You need people around you whom you respect enough to take notice of when they tell you that you are trying to run before you can walk. These could also be your professional advisors, but *you may need to ask someone to monitor you and give you honest feedback.*

Intensive Care

So you've been pinned down, your bike is locked firmly away, and your treatment continues! During your stay here you may need the following:

DRIPS

Unless you are a supremely arrogant kind of person, the chances are that now you will be beginning to need an extra boost of *self-esteem*. I have just been listening to Christopher Reeve (see page 136) on the radio talking about the embarrassment he began to feel at this stage. Looking back he could see that this was an inappropriate emotion. He had nothing to be embarrassed about. He had had an accident while doing something that he had made sure he was well equipped and well qualified to do.

I could relate to this feeling because I had it also a couple of years ago. I ended up in hospital with a head injury after fainting from the pain of a slight knock to a kneecap with one of my training weights. It was a familiar feeling for me because, like Christopher Reeve disclosed, whenever things go wrong in my life, *even when I am not to blame* I am likely to feel embarrassed and silly. Many people I know, for a whole variety of personal and cultural reasons, also have this response. It is one that has been preconditioned into our brains and will inevitably surface when we are functioning in emergency emotional mode.

During your Intensive Care phase it is particularly important to remember *not* to make the situation worse by putting yourself down for having these kind of 'silly responses'. Instead, put the limited energy you have into giving yourself a self-esteem boost.

If you cannot engage in the kind of activities I listed earlier on pages 111–112, try to ensure that the people around you are self-esteem builders and not the opposite kind (e.g. people who thrive on giving *'I told you so'* or *'Next time be careful ...'* lectures). If someone does start to affect your self-esteem in a negative way, just tell them. Much more often than not people are horrified to realize that they have done this and will then give you a massive 'drip feed' of genuine good feedback.

Don't forget that your role is to sit back and just accept the feed and not to try and pull out the tubes (e.g. *'Yes but, I wish I hadn't been so stupid.'* or *'Thanks, but most of the time I know I am a misery to be with'*).

DILIGENT NURSING

This is a time when you are very fragile and need to be con-stantly monitored and cared for. Your physical health will need building up, so make sure that you eat nourishing, easily digested food and possibly take extra vitamins. Allow yourself to be dependent for a while. Let other people cook and care for you and suppress any tendency to refuse offers (*'Thanks we're fine, we'll manage now'*). During our recent serious setbacks when our neighbours both in England and Spain visited our house with meals and tidied and washed for us, we were not only being physically cared for in a way which neither I nor my family would have bothered to do at the time, we were being psychologically nurtured. Their *practical acts of kindness* fed our spirits when we were in the very depths of despair and could not hear much comfort in words.

If such nursing is not offered, *try asking for it.* Many people don't help in these situations either because they don't want to interfere or disturb you, or simply because they have not thought of doing so. Society has become very isolated for most people. We are living busy lives in our separated boxes with our families scattered many miles away. But few people actu-ally *want* to live like this, even if they don't get around to doing much about it. If you present them with an opportunity to be neighbourly, they may jump at the chance. You can see this happen the moment there is a major communal disaster. People flock to help the hurt and traumatized, because sud-denly they feel they have the 'permission' to do so. (They seize the opportunity to feed their spirit though Servitude!)

PEACE AND QUIET

Having encouraged you to take help, I now want to remind you that you also need to have peace and quiet. Emotional traumas are very physically exhausting for the mind and the body. So once again, don't forget you can ask for it. You ask the chatterboxes to come back a little later when you will need and welcome their input.

Similarly, for the moment, keep yourself insulated from work pressures, however indispensable you think you are. Hibernation is what you need at this stage. Animals give it to themselves instinctively. I have been watching our normally high-spirited dog over the last day or two. He has taken to his bed. He is recovering from the trauma of my daughter's return to London after the Christmas holiday. When he first started to adopt these habits when he felt 'deserted', I worried and tried to 'jolly' him out of it very unsuccessfully. Now I have learned to leave him to 'nurse' his psychological wounds in peace and quiet.

METICULOUS MONITORING

I am also aware that some animals, like humans, do drift into *a physiological depressed state after a major loss* and may need treatment from a vet, so I will keep monitoring my dog's emotional state. I will watch to see when his appetite improves and when his normal enthusiasm for play returns. This is, of course, just what you need to do for yourself (or have done for you) after a major setback. Even the most normally upbeat people can suffer major depression and this is a condition which can be seriously life-threatening and is very easy to treat, especially in its *early* stages. The start of many chronic depressive illnesses can be traced back to a severe setback which wasn't given enough healing psychological attention at the time.

DIANA PRINCESS OF WALES 1961–1997

The story of Diana's life was one of almost continual setback after setback from her early childhood through to her tragic death. Though she of course enjoyed rare privileges, her difficult metamorphosis from a naïve, mousy caterpillar to a fragile tormented butterfly of breathtaking beauty was witnessed by the whole world. But, for a few years before her death, she seemed securely set to become a triumphant Thriver and an inspiring role model for sufferers of both external and internal struggles.

Treatment

Now you are out of danger territory. You should have some energy and be feeling like engaging with the world a little more. You will be wanting to 'get better' and start looking at ways to make a success out of this setback. But before you start on the action plan, make sure that you don't need either of the following:

CONFRONTATION

This is the time when the doctor faces us fairly and squarely with facts which he may have temporarily needed to hide from us.

Your own psychological defence system might have automatically put you into *denial*

> Every thing that happens to you is your teacher. The secret is to learn to sit at the feet of your own life and be taught by it.
>
> POLLY BERIEN BERENDS

mode as an emergency precaution while you were in Casualty and Intensive Care. After a major setback, we may need to stay in a state of stunned shock until we have the strength to face the pain. But now you have emerged from your protected cocoon you must look at *what has happened and what the consequences might be.* Ideally, you should have someone to help you to do this. This person should be a *friend or colleague who is assertive, honest and in control of their own pain and suffering* if indeed they currently have any.

If you haven't such a friend, you can always use a professional such as a counsellor, vicar, undertaker, solicitor or personnel manager for this purpose. Sometimes it is hard for the people who are in your 'family' to do this – they may, quite understandably, be too protective or too emotionally involved themselves. (I was pretty useless for my daughter and husband when Laura died, but I did encourage them to see other friends and professionals.)

Instant Workout – My Confrontative Friends

Make a note of any friends or professionals you currently know who could fulfil this role for you. If you do not know any, you have learned that you must start enquiring!

EMOTIONAL HEALING TIME

This is when the tears start to flow or the frustration and anger begin to mount as the truth of our 'injury' or 'disablement' hits us. We are often not very pleasant to be around at visiting time!

For the sake of your psychological health, you may need to work through some Emotional Healing! While you are on the treatment ward you may well be able to complete all the five essential stages of the strategy.

Every   Emotional   Cut   Can   Produce   Creative   Fruit

Essential Stages

1   Exploration – talking or writing about what has happened.
2   Expression – letting go of the feelings in some physical form.
3   Comfort – from an empathic person who respects our feelings and doesn't demand us to feel something we do not.
4   Compensation – finding some recompense for what has happened.
5   Perspective – seeing our emotional wound in the context of our life in general and/or the context of the problems of the universe!

Bonus Stages

6   Channelling – putting the learning from the experience into constructive use.
7   Forgiveness – for a contrite 'other' or ourselves.

If you can't complete these stages until later, you could at least begin planning now how you are going to monitor yourself through them. This will give you a boost anyway.

Finally, don't forget that they must *all* be worked through – and in the *right order*, even if there is some overlap.

Instant Workout – Emotional Healing

Close this book for a moment and see if you can remember the Emotional Healing strategy mnemonic sentence and the seven stages.

MEDICATION

You may need to take some tried-and-tested medicine that has worked for you in the past, but you may also need to experiment with a little of the new stuff now available.

Now is the time to get out some of your *favourite books and tapes* which have helped you to get back on your feet either psychologically or practically before. Alternatively, visit the library or bookstore (or find someone else to do this) and look for some *new, relevant titles*. Every week something is being published on one setback situation or other. Alternatively, for the latest information you may want to contact a *professional advisory body or self-help group, or search the Internet* for news and views.

Don't worry at this stage about making decisions – just flood yourself with information and new ideas while continuing to take it very easy.

Rehabilitation

Now you should be looking forward and outward rather than backward and inward. This is where you might get regular visits from the medical social worker and the physiotherapist to check that you are aware that discharge from hospital is imminent, and it's time to get thinking about how you are going to return to the world! So you may need to think about giving yourself:

SKILLS PRACTICE

After a major setback, we often suffer a loss of confidence. We find that we are afraid to do the simplest tasks, such as:

- ringing the employment or benefits agency
- filling out a bank loan or insurance application
- complaining about 'rough' or unfair treatment.

This would be the time to read through the PROACT strategy in this book (pages 171–173) and brush up on any of the skills which you may need.

It may be helpful to do some role-playing if, for example, you have a tough interview coming up. After a major setback we cannot have too much help in these areas. It is not worth taking any risks. The last thing you need is an unnecessary setback, so play safe and ask a friend to help give you some practice. Don't let embarrassment or fear of what others may think stop you from asking for what you need. (You can show the extent of your gratitude later!)

PRESCRIPTION AND/OR AFTERCARE PLAN

Usually after a major physical trauma we need some aftercare help on discharge. After a setback, this is your step-by-step action plan, the securing of necessary resources and the making of arrangements with a friend or professionals for support and monitoring.

Instant Workout – Aftercare

- Read the Positive Action Strategy on pages 165–167 and the PROACT Strategy on pages 171–173.
- Close this book and test yourself by trying to recall the names of all the stages of both strategies.

Convalescence

The concept of convalescence in the realm of physical treatment has almost earned its place in the history books. We are so anxious to remove people from hospital and back into a full life at work and the community that this last treatment stage is more often than not skipped. Convalescent homes in the country and by the seaside are now almost extinct.

I shall refrain from commenting on the wisdom of this development in the field of physical health, and confine myself to the field which I know more about! My view is that a period of convalescence after a major setback is *essential if you want to be a Thriver and make a success out of your experience.* You must cycle along the flat, peaceful lanes until you have restored your confidence and have faith in your ability to tackle the mountain routes.

But you do not have to isolate yourself for a period, *just gently ease yourself back into normal, everyday life.* If you have to return to work full-time (and most of us do), then make sure that you give yourself as easy a time as is possible at home and in your social life.

If you don't take it easy at first, you run the risk of making a mistake because it is unlikely that you will be functioning at your best, even though you may think you are. I can fully understand the impatience to get back into a full life in the fast lane (it helps us temporarily to forget the pain). I have done it many times myself. But I have learned through personal hindsight and through helping others that it does not pay to do so in the long run. People who can dive into the deep end after a major setback are the exception, not the rule.

So, if you are tempted, ask yourself these questions:

- Do I really need to take this risk?
- Who am I trying to please or impress by playing tough?
- Do I want to be a Survivor or a Thriver?

> What doesn't kill me makes me stronger.
>
> ALBERT CAMUS
>
> I believe that it's what you do after a disaster that can give it meaning.
>
> CHRISTOPHER REEVE

CHRISTOPHER REEVE 1952–

Christopher was born in the US and became an international film star in the role of Superman. Although his childhood was not economically deprived it was full of emotional upheaval. As a young adult he also lost two of his close friends in different sporting accidents and had several near-misses himself. When he first had the serious riding accident which has left him paralysed, he says he immediately thought 'I'll be OK, everything's fine. I've survived a lot of difficult situations before, both physically and emotionally.' Despite many setbacks and periods of deep despair and self-doubt during the last three years, he is proving himself to be stunningly right. Even though he is unable to move or breathe by himself, he has written a brilliant book; directed a film; given **countless inspiring lectures and broadcasts; raised enormous funds for similarly disabled but disadvantaged people, and personally motivated many individual sufferers. He has also been responsible for dramatically accelerating the pace of research into spinal injury to the point where it is now so advanced that he may make a physical recovery.**

CHAPTER 7

Helping Others
Make a Success
of Setbacks

Feeling the need to help after seeing someone experience a setback is an instinctive, natural response. We are social animals and our emotions have evolved to enable us to bond together.

> To know even one life has breathed easier because you have lived, this is to have succeeded.
> RALPH WALDO EMERSON

The development of the universe has reached a stage when human beings *need* to work together to make further progress. When one of us is hurt and in trouble, we therefore feel pain and want to help. For the survival of humankind, and not just our consciences and self-esteem, we need to help each other thrive after a setback.

But the reality is that, although we may feel the feeling of our instinctive response, fewer and fewer people are acting upon it. The reasons are many and complicated. We may be too stressed ourselves or too busy. But more and more often nowadays I hear people saying it isn't these reasons that stop them from helping, it is that they don't know **what** would help or **how** they should give this help.

They do nothing for fear of doing the wrong thing!

At the very best, they may call in a professional helper and stand helplessly by in awe of that person's special gift or expertise.

How sad! What a waste of human love and potential!

It is so *easy* to make a difference to someone going through a setback, and we can derive so much pleasure and satisfaction from so doing.

I have written this following list of tips and suggestions, but I know it is far from being complete. There are so many other ways to help, as anyone who has ever been through a setback knows only too well. I feel very strongly that we must stop robbing ourselves of this instinctive human quality and reclaim our right to help each other, however quaintly or ineffectually we may do so.

I know I may be talking myself out of a job, but, as I have been saying for years, I'd be quite happy to run a tea room if ever that dream should come to pass!

Tips to Help You Help!

JUST *BE* THERE

Trust that you can play a vital role. Never underestimate the good you can do, even just by showing your support by your physical presence. The person having the setback (especially if it is major) may not appear to notice you or even thank you, but most are very appreciative later and say how important that 'show' of support was.

LISTEN ATTENTIVELY

This is often all they need! Once again it may sometimes feel as though you are doing nothing, but you are really helping. You can make your role even more effective by following the guidelines on page 147. After a setback, even the greatest orators are sometimes tongue-tied. By using these tips you can play a great role in helping them to talk. Talking is one of the most important ways of healing from an emotional wound, and is obviously a very useful way of trying to analyse the confusion in our minds and make decisions. Being an effective listener is probably one of the best ways of empowering people, as any counsellor or good manager knows. In the long run it is much more effective than instructing people about what they ought to do!

ADVISE RARELY AND, WHEN YOU DO, ASK PERMISSION

Try to keep your advice first for emergencies when the person may be too emotionally upset to think for themselves. And secondly, for the later stages when they are planning action, but at that time it is important to ask permission before giving it. And when you do give it, avoid using the words 'should' or 'ought'. Use 'would' or 'could' instead.

> Each player must accept the cards life deals him or her: but once they are in hand, he or she alone must decide how to play the cards in order to win the game.
>
> VOLTAIRE

- ✗ *You should go into his office and just give him hell!*
- ✓ *Would you like to hear what ideas I have?*
- ✓ *I think you'd be justified in going into his office and letting him know directly how he has hurt you.*
- ✓ *You could let him know you are angry and then he may ...*

SHARE, BUT DON'T ASSUME

When we hear about a setback, we often immediately think of one or more of our similar experiences. It may be helpful for the other person to hear about these because they will then feel less isolated, and they may even pick up a good tip or two or find a buried feeling within themselves that they had not acknowledged. But be careful not to generalize from your experience and assume that your way of reacting or making a success is the same as theirs.

✗   *You ought to have a good cry. I did when ...*

✓   *When I was in a similar situation, I know I felt very sad and I felt loads better when I let it all out one day. But everyone, I know, can react differently.*

✗   *I don't think any couple can really be friends after a divorce. I thought we could, but as soon as we ...'*

✓   *I know how you feel because when I became divorced I was determined to stay friends. We didn't manage it, but maybe you will.*

HOLD BACK ON THE JUDGEMENTS

I am reluctant to put this tip in because I am sure that I am preaching to the converted! We all know (if only from personal experience!) that it is not helpful to hear 'I told you so' or 'You should ...' comments in the aftermath of a setback, *but* how many of us still hear ourselves doing this? It is often our panic that makes us react in this way. We are probably acting on auto-pilot (maybe this is what people did to us after a setback when we were little).

> If you find you have started to be judgemental, just apologize and offer to do something comforting or constructive. Your wisdom is much more likely to be appreciated at a later stage.

GIVE PRACTICAL HELP

If you are choking on your frustration and have 'swallowed' your good advice, instead use your energy to do something practical to show support, even if the other person doesn't really need it. Good deeds after a setback commonly have more symbolic than practical value. Don't always feel you have to have their permission for this though, especially soon after the setback.

✓ Just do it. Just remember that coping with a setback always requires extra energy, so if you can save them even a little you will be helping a good deal. (We are helping to build Thrivers, not just Survivors!)

✗ But of course, as they are starting to pick up, be careful not to smother their need to become independent again and feel that *they* are capable of making a success out of their setback.

For example you could:

✓ Collect information from the library or Internet.
✓ Make a cup of tea, do some shopping or mow their lawn.
✓ Take some of their more stressful work over (intercept and deal with that 'difficult' customer, patient or colleague).
✓ Give them a copy of this book or cassette, or one of its strategies or action plans!

WRITE DOWN YOUR SUPPORT

Even people who appear to be surrounded by plenty of love and support will appreciate reading and re-reading cards and letters. During the months after Laura's death I must have read all mine a hundred times over, and many were from people I had never met. Even three years later, I sometimes dip into the box where they sit with many other precious objects associated with Laura, and draw comfort. Christopher Reeve writes movingly about doing the same in *Still Me* (Century, 1998).

✗ Don't wait for the major tragedy before writing.
✓ Always keep some notelets or postcards at the ready, and develop the habit of sending a few words to people who are going through even 'minor' hard times. (Remember, it's success with the minors that helps us handle the majors!)

✓   If you cannot find the words yourself to express your feelings, find someone else who can. There are many books of quotations and inspiring or comforting cards around.

DRAW A PICTURE OR MAKE A GIFT

Some people are much better at expressing their support in a creative way without using words. I have been very appreciative of paintings and little drawings which have been done for me during difficult times. I was also lucky enough to have a wonderful bust of Laura made by a sculptor who hadn't even met her.

✗   Don't hold back just because you are not a Picasso – it truly is the thought which counts at these times.
✓   Try making or drawing something which can have symbolic significance as well. The message will stick so much more firmly in the brain than words expressing the same sentiment. If it will raise a smile, that's even better. (You don't need an art degree to do a pin-drawing of someone submerged under a pile of loaves of bread to say 'Good luck with asking for the loan!')

GIVE THEM SOME APPROPRIATE MUSIC

Music is also a powerful means of communication when words are difficult to find. It is one of the most effective ways of changing a mood. Many people I know find that they need different kinds of music after a setback, so a CD or tape of music they don't normally listen to could be very welcome. For example, you could bring soothing music, uplifting tunes or songs to elicit suppressed feelings, depending on their need.

✗   Don't force your musical tastes on them by just playing music without their consent (e.g. to cheer them up!)

✓ Take a risk – buy or lend them a CD or tape to play on their own.

JOSÉ CARRERAS 1946–

José was born in Spain. At the age of two he nearly drowned and was only saved by receiving mouth-to-mouth resuscitation from his mother. José was devastated when she died from cancer 16 years later. Throughout his childhood she had devoted herself to making his dream of becoming a singer come true. When he developed leukaemia, and throughout other setbacks in his life, he says that he 'derived courage and confidence' from recalling her faith in him. Since his remarkable comeback after his illness he has set up a highly successful leukaemia foundation and believes his singing has greatly improved. He says, 'The experience has given me a deeper understanding of the music.'

GIVE THEM OPPORTUNITIES TO BE USEFUL

As they progress on from the initial stages of shock, one of the best ways to fan the potential Thriver flames is to empower them by allowing them to be of use in some way or other. This does not have to be related to their setback. Ideally it should also be an opportunity for them to use their strengths, but it does not have to be.

✗ Don't patronize them by giving them useless tasks. There is always something that even people disabled from the severest setbacks can achieve. (Read Christopher Reeve's or Jean-Dominique Bauby's books if you need convincing! – see Further Reading.)

✓ Let them help you, even by just listening. For example: When you visit them, share your problems and then thank them and say how useful it was having a chance to talk things over.

✓   Select tasks that they can easily achieve until they have their confidence back.

SHOW YOUR SUPPORT FINANCIALLY

Even if the person with a setback may not need your help, others in similar circumstances might. It is very healing for anyone going through a tough time to know that their experience has helped others. Even the tiniest donations to Laura's Foundation have had an enormous strengthening impact on us, but there doesn't necessarily have to be a special charity.

✓   For example, if they have been robbed, let them know you have sent a donation to Victim Support; if they have been diagnosed with arthritis, let them know you have suggested the proceeds of the School Fair are sent to an arthritis charity.

SOAK UP THEIR ANGER OR GRIEF, BUT NOT UNTIL YOU ARE SOGGY

If they show an inclination to cry or let out some irritation, just imagine that you are a sponge. You don't have to do anything but absorb it and stop it from turning back inwards or spilling over elsewhere.

✗   Don't let your sponge become too full.
✓   Make sure you wring it out as soon as you can, and find some way of relieving your tension or letting go of the feelings you have absorbed.
✓   Let the other person know if you have had enough for the moment. That is better than pretending you can take anything and still stand upright. When a person has had a setback, their sensitivity to other's pain or needs can be hampered. They may not know how much you can take and would welcome your being honest. They will find it so much easier to be with you if they know you are taking responsibility for looking after *yourself*.

✓ Remember that there are many other highly absorbent sponges in the world even if you haven't met them yet! Just put out an SOS and they will come running.

MAKE THEM LAUGH, BUT NOT TOO EARLY

'Laughing off' or 'laughing away' a setback is not what a Thriver should be doing. That would be dismissing it as unimportant and therefore useless. But, at the right time, humour can play a great part in helping to relieve tension and seeing the experience in some perspective.

✗ Keep the wise-cracks to yourself.
✓ Do little tests (the odd joke) to see if the person is ready for a big dose of fun.

KEEP MONITORING THEIR PATH TO SUCCESS

Often immediately after a setback, especially a major one, people do have enough support. However, it is in the later stages when they are plodding along with their action plan and perhaps are meeting mini-hurdles that they sometimes need encouragement even more. It is so easy to forget when life seems to have settled back into a normal routine.

✓ Make a note in your diary to remind you to make a call just to 'see how things are going'.
✓ Be confrontative if they are being unrealistic or are sinking into denial or a 'poor me' mode.
✗ Never assume that anyone is above this kind of help!

> Have you learned lessons only of those who admired you, and were tender with you, and stood aside for you? Have you not learned great lessons from those who braced themselves against you, and disputed the passage with you?
>
> WALT WHITMAN

GIVE REWARDS AND HELP CELEBRATE SUCCESS

Not just when they have reached their final goal, but when they are struggling in the early stages as well.

- ✓ Make sure that the reward is appropriate to the task they have completed or the amount of effort they have put in, but in *their* eyes, not yours. What is success to you may not be the same to them.
- ✓ Insist that they give themselves the rewards they have planned when they were goal-setting. Don't let them say that meeting with success is now enough. Thrivers need as much positive reinforcement as the world can provide!

BE AN INSPIRING ROLE-MODEL

If you want someone to 'Cheer-up' or 'Get motivated', the very best thing you can do is DEMONSTRATE! Obviously, if you have read this book you will appreciate that the time and place to do this is rarely in the immediate aftermath of a setback. (Some major setbacks may be exceptions.)

- ✓ If you are doing this regularly (and the emotional effects of some people's setbacks last for years), think about getting support from a self-help group or professional organization. Many of these now have special sections for 'carers', not just sufferers, as we are now so aware of the damaging effect of being a sponge for extended periods without support.
- ✓ Improve your own ability to become a Thriver and make success from setbacks!

> There's only one corner of the universe you can be certain of improving, and that's your own self ... You have to begin there, not outside not on other people. That comes afterwards, when you've worked on your own corner.
>
> ALDOUS HUXLEY

How to Listen to Someone Who Has Just Had a Setback

Show respect for their own opinion on the seriousness of the setback, even if you disagree.

✗   *Stop worrying. You're taking it too seriously.*
✓   *I appreciate it seems very serious to you, but maybe I can help you.*

Show empathy for *their* emotional response and don't expect them to feel what you would feel, even though you feel compelled to share your emotional reaction.

✗   *You shouldn't feel upset – he hurt you. You should feel angry.*
✓   *I can understand why you are upset and feel hurt, although I am feeling angry on your behalf with him.*

Hold back on interrupting unnecessarily with your **'own story'** when something the speaker says jogs a memory or idea of your own.

✗   *Yes, that happened to me too. Last week when I was trying to .....*

Use **encouraging noises**, words and phrases freely to indicate that you are paying attention:

✓   *Mmm; Oh!; Really? That's interesting.*

Show your attention also through your **own body language**:

✓   Nod; make some direct eye-contact; smile; sit *slightly* forward.

If they are becoming hesitant and you want to encourage their flow, **repeat key words** and phrases which they have just used. (You don't even have to put them in a sentence.)

If they are going around in circles, to get the conversation back on a more constructive track you can interrupt firmly (with a hand gesture if necessary) and **refer back** to phrases or words which *they* have used.

> ✓ *Can I just go back to what you said just now? You said you were thinking of ...*

From time to time and at the end of your conversation, **summarize** what you think you have heard them say. People in highly emotional states tend to have unreliable memories and may not have expressed themselves accurately.

> ✓ *Could I just stop you for a moment and check what I think I've heard you say?*

Sometimes it can be very helpful to use a **metaphor** which seems to sum up the essence of the message which you think that they are trying to convey.

> ✓ *Do you feel you are lost in a desert with no one to help?*

Synchronize your body language with theirs as closely as possible. Check you are not, for example, smiling (to cheer them up!) if they are frowning; speaking fast when they need to speak slowly; sitting very casually when they are bolt upright; staring when they are avoiding eye-contact.

If you need more information, check that you are using **open questions** to ensure that you receive more than a one-word response. These will usually begin with one of the following:

> ✓ What, why, where, who, when and how

Ask **closed questions** when you want the speaker to move on from one subject to another (people who have had a setback are not usually at their most succinct!), for example:

✓   *Do you think that we've covered all the different possibilities? ... Good. So perhaps we could move on to ...?*
✓   *Which of these two options do you prefer?*
✓   *Are you pleased with what we have decided?*

Check out the messages you are picking up from **their body language**; don't assume you can read it.

✓   *I notice you tapping your finger ... I was wondering if you're feeling angry as well as sad ...?*
✓   *I saw you glance at your watch, are you worried about the time?*

Avoid rushing in to fill every **silence**. Remember that some people need to pause frequently to clarify their thinking before speaking, and after a setback we all need more time to think than usual.

Avoid rushing with **unnecessary good advice, reassurances or 'cheer-up' humour**, as this can stop them from finding *their own* solution and may block emotional healing.

✗   *Let's look on the bright side, you could be dead.*
✗   *If I were you ...*
✗   *In a month's time you'll have forgotten all this.*

OPRAH WINFREY 1954–

Oprah survived a traumatic childhood, which included being sexually abused and sentenced to a detention centre at 13. She was then sent to live with her father, who was a strict disciplinarian, making her write a report on a book she had read each week. In her subsequent career as the world's most famous TV host, she has publicized inspiring personal development books. She made the knowledge within these books available to millions of people who would not otherwise have been able to benefit from them. She became the first woman in history to own and produce her own TV show, and through her charitable work has transformed the lives of many thousands of other people from disadvantaged and abusive backgrounds.

CHAPTER 8

 Strategies

and

Guidelines

Emotional Skills

CONTROLLING ANXIETY

First unlock your physical tension by uncrossing your arms and legs and putting both feet flat on the floor, and then screwing up your fingers and toes and slowly releasing three times.

Alternatively, do 2 to 3 minutes of your favourite stretching exercises – or you could run on the spot for 1 minute. If you are still tense, do this next exercise. It can be used literally anywhere, such as sitting in a waiting area or a car park, but it works even better if you can find somewhere to lie down or sit in a lotus-style position (cross-legged).

Magic Mental Reviver

Close your eyes. Consciously relax any tension in your body. Check that your face, jaw, hands, arms, legs and feet are loose, and allow yourself to sink into, and feel supported by, whatever surface you are sitting or lying on.

Take three or four slow deep breaths, while mentally following the passage of your breath as it goes in and out (sometimes it helps to imagine it as one colour as it is drawn in, and another as it is expelled).

Now let yourself breathe naturally and easily, while slowly counting backwards from 50, or repeating the alphabet like this: ab, bc, cd, de, ef, etc. Each time a thought comes back into your mind, return to the start and begin again!

Finish with a few moments of allowing your mind to just gently float.

Repeat, if you have time.

Scenic Symbol Meditation

Relax yourself, again as above.

Close your eyes and focus your mind's eye on a chosen symbol or scene which conjures up an image of success or a feeling of peace and relaxation (e.g. a handshake, a goal being scored, a sunset on the beach, or the face of someone whom you admire immensely).

Use your imagination to examine your symbol in minute detail. Every time a thought comes into your head, re-focus your mind's eye onto the symbol for 1–5 minutes.

CONTROLLING FEAR

Positive Affirmation Meditation

Relax yourself as above.

With your eyes closed, say a very short appropriate affirmation sentence as you breathe in and out (e.g. While breathing in: 'I am'; as you breathe out: '… confident/in control/ courageous/capable', etc.).

As thoughts, worries or ruminations come into your mind, gently return the focus of your mind to your chosen affirmation for 1–5 minutes.

The 'Night Before' Pacifier

This creative visualization technique uses your imagination to help you rehearse your confidence skills. It will also feed your subconscious with an empowering positive image of you successfully achieving your goal with the minimum amount of stress.

When to use it:

The evening before you have to face a difficult challenge, throughout which it is important for you to both feel and appear calm and confident. The exercise will take between 20 minutes and 1 hour, depending on how much time you can spare (the longer the better!). You could have some gently relaxing music on in the background.

What you do:

Note down concisely on several cards:

- Your main objectives (checking that they are achievable as well as challenging).
- Three adjectives which would summarize the overall image you intend to present.
- The warning signals of your main personal sabotage patterns which may get in the way of you achieving your objectives.
- The 'worst case scenario', and note down your contingency plan for coping with and recovering from it.
- The rewards (both long-term and short-term) you will gain from your success, and an outline plan for celebration and/or support.

Lie in a place where you can be private and undisturbed (the bath?), and spend 5 to 10 minutes deeply relaxing your body to the stage where your mind has reached the 'floating' stage.

Staying relaxed and breathing rhythmically and gently, take your imagination to the time when you are due to wake up the next morning. Visualize yourself getting dressed and generally preparing for your day in a positive, relaxed manner. Watch yourself enjoying a favourite nurturing breakfast while calmly reading through the cards you prepared last night.

Continue to visualize yourself hour-by-hour proceeding *successfully* through the events of your day. Take care to get a picture of yourself looking cool, calm and collected throughout any crisis or difficult time which may come into your mind. Notice and admire your assertive body language, and use your mind's ear to listen to the authoritative, controlled tones of your voice.

Finally, visualize yourself enjoying a reward (and/or celebration) for your achievement. Stay with your vision of the successful 'you' for as long as you can, because the stronger this image is, the more likely it is to become translated into reality the next day!

CONTROLLING ANGER

'Don't Get Too Boiling': A Quick-fix Strategy for Our Own Anger

This strategy should be used as soon as you feel your own anger is beginning to take a physical hold (e.g. your pulse quickening, muscles tightening, head throbbing, etc.). This mnemonic sentence will help you learn the four steps off by heart.

D on't	G et	T oo	B oiling
I	R	E	R
S	O	N	E
T	U	S	A
A	N	I	T
N	D	O	H
C		N	E
E			

Distance

Let go immediately of any physical contact you may have (especially if it is with a person!). Take a step back or lean back in chair. Alternatively, leave the room for a few minutes. This is a primitive 'I'm backing off' response, and is used by all animals who want to stop fighting, so it sends a quick signal to your brain (and to the brain of anyone else who has produced a fight response).

Ground

Take hold of some firm inanimate object to help bring yourself back 'down to earth'.

Then switch your brain into its left-brain logical mode. (The right brain is where your emotions are processed). Some examples of quick ways to do this, if you cannot leave the scene, are to count silently all the objects in the room of the same colour, or the number of circles you can see. Alternatively you could list the ingredients for tonight's recipe, or call to mind today's news headlines.

If you can take a break away, spend 5–15 minutes doing a distracting mundane chore, which requires some thought, such as filing or reorganizing a cupboard, or writing a Christmas present list.

Tension

Do something which will release the build-up of physical tension. You could surreptitiously clench and unclench fists, curl and uncurl toes or, if you have some privacy, you could screw your face up and slowly release the muscles, or you could thump a cushion. You could also kick a ball, swim a mile or have a good scream.

Breathe

Finally, before returning to deal with the situation, use a deep breathing exercise to calm your pulse. Then make sure that you continue to take one or two deep slow breaths for at least the next 5 minutes.

Communication Skills

SELF-PROMOTION – THE THREE PREPARATION TASKS

1 Prepare Your Image

People listen more to those who are 'easy on the eye' and wear appropriate clothes. If we jar the eyes of our beholders, we may not do ourselves justice. In the heat of a setback, it is easy to let our appearance deteriorate, because attending to it slips understandably down our priority list. This might in fact be the best time to treat yourself to a new outfit, hairstyle or a visit to an image consultant, because your self-esteem could probably do with the boost as well.

2 Prepare the Content

At the very least, think through what you are going to say, including any responses you might want to make to criticisms or objections. After a setback, we are often in 'hurry up' mode, and it is tempting to skip this preparatory step because we want to get into action as soon as possible. But it is even more important to take time out to think through, write out and rehearse what you want to say, because your brain might not be functioning as well as it normally does. Emotions such as guilt or low self-esteem after making a mistake, or anger after being let-down, can disrupt our logical thinking processes. Use the Scripting Technique (see my book *Assert Yourself*) to help you at least prepare your opening speech.

3 Prepare Your Inner Psychological State

It is important to project a confident manner from within. Research has shown that people listen more to those who present themselves with calm confidence. After a setback, even the most confident people often need a boost. You can obtain this by spending some time before your event with a close friend, or you could use the following strategy.

TAKE A DOSE OF COURAGE

This is a preparation strategy for controlling anxiety and boosting confidence.

It can be used to prepare yourself psychologically for any difficult situation. It can be especially useful if you are nervous or lacking in confidence about going for an interview, 'selling' a solution to a problem to a critical, cynical audience, or re-embarking on a difficult challenge at which you may have failed previously.

The first letters of the mnemonic sentence remind us of each key step.

Take	A	Dose	Of	Courage
Tranquillity	Affirmation	Decision	Outcome	Courage

Tranquillity

- Ten minutes before starting, take yourself to a tranquil place for 3–5 minutes – at least.
- Find a quiet room, garden, back yard or even a corridor. Failing this, you can usually make an excuse to go to the loo!
- Wherever you are, close your eyes and mentally remove yourself to one of your favourite peaceful locations.
- First take a moment to *physically* calm yourself. If you are in a private place, do some tension release exercises – slowly bending and stretching your legs and arms. Lift your shoulders to your ears and slowly roll them back and down. Move your head gently from side to side and up and down. Then screw up all your facial muscles including pressing your tongue against your palette, then slowly release. Gently waggle your jaw from side to side. Push your lips forward several times.
- Finally, take three or four deep, slow breaths. Then, using your mind's eye, look around your chosen peaceful location – allowing yourself, for at least 1 minute, to sense its tranquillity and enjoy its peace.

Affirmations

Affirmations are short, positive, present-tense statements.

Repeat a few well-chosen sentences over and over again, preferably out loud. For the purposes of this step you might say to yourself: *I am calm and in control; I enjoy interviews; I am an excellent speaker; I am confident; I can succeed this time.*

If you have never used affirmations before, you'll be surprised at how effective this kind of simple self-talk is – remember the part of your brain controlling your conditioned anxiety response is a primitive structure. It responds best to straight talking – it cannot respond to lengthy sermons and rational explanations.

Decision

A common response to setbacks is to start resenting the fact that *we* have to pick up the pieces. We start to believe that we are being forced to do whatever we need to do (e.g. retype a letter/ask for another loan/find a new job or friend). We tend to feel like victims of the situation, and victims do not usually ooze coolness and confidence!

So the point of this step is to remind yourself that, unless you literally have a gun to your head, you are not powerless – even if your emotional brain has jumped to that erroneous conclusion. You *can* choose to act or not act, and you *can* choose to do it with or without confidence.

Switch yourself into an empowered mode by saying several times in a calm, firm voice: *I have decided to ... and I will do it with calmness and confidence.*

Outcome

You are now going to motivate yourself even more by focusing your mind on a successful result.

List on paper what you stand to gain if you succeed. Don't forget that when doing a visualization, it is always much more effective if you can bring it alive *emotionally*. Therefore try to feel the feelings which accompany the image which you create in your mind. So, as you are seeing yourself enjoying your success, physically feel the glow of confidence or pleasure.

Courage

Once again, you'll need your imagination.

Bring to mind the faces of two or three people whose persistent courage you have admired. These could be people who are currently alive or who could be dead. They could even be people whom you have never met, such as sports heroes who have overcome setbacks, or imaginary characters from the world of films or fiction.

Imagine that they are standing in front of you and encouraging you. Note the expression in their eyes. Listen carefully to the words or phrases they use – hear their supportive tone of voice. Courage undoubtedly has infectious properties – so make these work for you – bring your heroes' courage to life by giving it some imaginary form and colour – and then, watch yourself being infected – picture their courage flowing freely and directly into the centre of your heart. Again, allow yourself to sense physically the feeling this visualization stimulates.

If you begin to lose courage again, when you are in your situation just recall the image of your heroes and your emotional brain should switch off its alarm bells and allow you to continue with renewed confidence.

> I felt fear myself more times than I can remember, but I hid it under a mask of boldness. The brave man is not he who does not feel afraid, but he who conquers that fear.
>
> NELSON MANDELA

JEAN-DOMINIQUE BAUBY 1952-1997

Jean-Dominique was born in France and had a successful career as a journalist. At the age of 43 he suffered a stroke which left him completely paralysed and speechless. Using incredible reserves of courage and persistence he found a way of communicating by blinking his left eye-lid, which was the only part of him he could move. He persevered through incredible setbacks of pain and humiliating experiences to write (by blinking his eye to a secretary) what has been described by many renowned critics as 'one of the great books of the century'. This book is enabling people for the first time to appreciate and understand the subjective experiences of patients suffering from the 'locked-in' syndrome.

FOGGING – A TECHNIQUE TO STOP THE FLOW OF
UNWANTED CRITICISM

In the immediate aftermath of a setback, we often feel fragile. Although a Thriver is someone who welcomes constructive feedback on their failures and mistakes, for a while your priority might be to rest and heal. When you are feeling strong enough, you can then *invite* feedback which you think might help you to learn from the setback.

This technique will stop the flow of criticism until you are ready to ask for it. The guidelines following it will help you to make sure that what you hear is as constructive and potentially helpful as possible.

Instead of defending yourself, you can just respond to your critic by *calmly* saying that there *may be some truth* in what they are saying (while *inwardly* reserving your right to take time to consider or disagree). For example:

You could be right. Perhaps I could have talked it over with you before going ahead.

Yes, maybe I shouldn't have assumed so much about him.

You could have a point. If I had started revising a bit earlier, I might have passed.

Many people are afraid to use Fogging because it may *appear* that you are agreeing with the critic even when you are not. It is important to remember that the point of the technique is to give you *temporary* protection. If you want to challenge the criticism you can always do so at a later date (using the following guidelines, of course!).

HOW TO ASK FOR CONSTRUCTIVE CRITICISM

Here are 10 steps to ensure you obtain feedback which is useful – and which neither damages your image nor self-confidence.

1   **Calm yourself** – use deep breathing or one of the above control strategies to ensure that you are fully in charge of your emotions. It would be unusual if you did not feel some degree of anxiety or anger, but you must not allow these feelings to have the upper hand and make you overly passive or defensive.

2   **Explain why you want the feedback** – e.g. 'I know that I have made a mistake and I am anxious not to make it again' or 'You have known me many years and I value your opinions. So I thought you may be able to throw some honest light on why I didn't get the promotion.'

3   **Ask for positive as well as negative feedback** – especially if you know that your critic is longing for an opportunity to attack you! For example, say 'I know that you feel there are many things that I could have done differently. I certainly want to hear about this, but I would also appreciate it if you could let me know whether I did anything right as well.'

4   **Request *specific* examples** – ask your critic to give times and dates and examples of what, in their opinion, you failed to do or say, or said or did incorrectly or ineptly.

5   **Deflect personal attacks and put-downs immediately** – if they start attacking your character, rather than specific aspects of your *behaviour*, stop them by saying, for example: 'Can I stop you for a minute, because I don't find

it helpful just to be told I'm lazy/too enthusiastic or unconfident – I would rather you gave me an example of the kind of behaviour or words that made you think that about me.'

6   **Ask for *constructive* suggestions** – say that you would find it helpful to have some ideas or practical advice, e.g. 'What do you think I could have done or said instead?' or 'What do you think I would be advised to do differently next time?'

7   **Summarize** – very commonly when we are receiving criticism, our anxiety prevents us from hearing and perceiving accurately. It is always a good idea to repeat back what you think your critic has said in a summarized form. This also helps the critic to feel better (most people are goodies and feel uncomfortable about hurting others!) and more motivated to give you feedback again. Thrivers want to know people who are willing to give honest and helpful opinions and advice. For example: 'So, if I have understood you correctly, you think I worked hard and it was a good idea, but I should have consulted a few more people before starting and taken more time to monitor my progress.'

8   **Thank** – all feedback is useful, even if some is more useful than others! So for example say: 'Thank you for taking the time to talk to me' or 'Thank you for being so forthright.'

9   **Share your action plan** – say what you intend to do as a result of listening to their feedback, e.g. 'I'd like to take some time to mull over what you have said and then decide what to do' or 'I'll certainly make sure that, next time, I start earlier.'

10   **Boost your self-esteem** – you are human! Criticism hurts even though it can be incredibly useful. Thrivers make sure that they don't forget their strengths and what they are capable of doing well. I know my own strengths have a tendency to slip my mind after a dose of criticism! So give yourself a treat or spend some time with someone who appreciates your worth (*but not* necessarily someone who feels compelled to reverse the good that your critic has done).

> When somebody says, 'I hope you won't mind my telling you this,' it's pretty certain that you will.
>
> SYLVIA BREMER

MAKING A DIFFICULT REQUEST

After setbacks such as failures or mistakes, we commonly find we are in a position of asking someone for a favour, or to give us a 'second chance', and this is not always easy to do in an assertive manner. I hope the following guidelines will be useful. But don't forget that they could also be used as a guide to making any kind of request at any time!

- Request a specific 'appointment' whenever possible – this is especially important if you think your request may require some time for discussion or negotiation. Even if your request is to a friend or family member, they will be more likely to be amenable if they don't feel put on the spot. Try also to state how long your discussion may take. For example: 'I want to ask you a favour, but I'd like some time to explain why. I know you are busy but could you spare 15 minutes sometime later today?'
- Prepare your request – do a *concise* summary of the background of your need and your request. (One or two sentences should usually be enough. Further information can be put on paper or given later. Long-winded justifications, especially at the outset, rarely help our cause!) If you are particularly anxious, rehearse making your request in front of a friend or the mirror. This will also give you an opportunity to check that you are using confident body language and that you don't sound whiny or pathetic – easy to do in the circumstances. You could further reinforce your confidence by doing a creative visualization, and feeding your brain with a positive image of your request being granted.

- Relax yourself – 5–10 minutes before, do some tension-release exercises. (Go to the loo and screw up your face and body and release a couple of times. Take four slow, deep breaths.) It is not a good idea to look anxious – it can make you seem desperate, even if you are not, and the other person could feel 'cornered' or manipulated.

- Assume confident body language – make sure that both feet are on the ground, you have an upright posture, your tone of voice is strong and that you have direct eye contact.

- Start positively – don't start by loading them with a long depressing bad luck story, or a diatribe about your previous failings, or suggesting that they may refuse you (e.g. 'You'll probably tell me to get lost, and I wouldn't blame you'). Instead, for example, say: 'I am hoping you can help me. I am keen to make a new start and …' or 'I am looking at ways of making the best of what happened and this is why …'

- Empathize – with their situation, difficulties or feelings. For example, 'I appreciate that you have helped many times before and may be feeling reluctant' or 'I know that you are short of time.'

- State your rehearsed request briefly and confidently – you can increase your chances of being refused if you over-elaborate or speak in a way which sounds as though you expect (or deserve!) to be refused.

- Say how pleased you would be to have your request considered or granted.

- Indicate gratitude – but don't fawn or grovel, or manipulate: 'I really appreciate you giving my request some consideration,' not 'I've chosen to ask you because I know you are a saint!'

- Conclude with an 'either/or' question – ask them when you could expect an answer to your request. For example: 'Would it be possible to give me an answer by Wednesday, or do you need a little longer to consider it?'

Organizational Skills

POSITIVE ACTION STRATEGY

After a setback, even if we are determined to overcome the problem, we often find it difficult to find a starting point. This strategy is designed to help you maintain your psychological strength as well as be realistic and down-to-earth in your planning.

It falls into four distinct parts, so I have created the following mnemonic as a reminder.

Good	**S**trategies	**R**eap	**S**uccess
Goals	**S**abotage	**R**esources	**S**upport

Goals

Long term:

> Outline your general objectives and what you would like to achieve in the distant future (1–5 years).

Short term:

> Name specific targets and outcomes you expect to see during the next six months.

Immediate action:

> Specify your plan for today or what you intend to do before the end of next week.

Sabotage

Own:

> Ask yourself 'How am I likely to stop myself achieving these goals?' (That is, specify your relevant bad habits!)

Others:

Ask yourself: 'Is there anyone else who may try either consciously or unconsciously to hinder me?' (Other people's attitudes and uncooperative behaviour.)

Action:

Specify what action you will take to counter both kinds of sabotage.

Resources

Own:

Ask yourself: 'What personal strengths, knowledge and skills do I have which could help me achieve my goals?'

Other:

Ask yourself: 'What other resources do I need?' (money; administrative back-up; expertise; equipment, etc.)

Action:

Specify what you are going to do in order to strengthen your current resources or acquire new ones.

Support

Current:

Ask yourself: 'Which of my friends or colleagues could give me appropriate support and which are currently available and willing to do so? Who could help me to monitor my progress most efficiently? Who could help me reward myself when I succeed?'

New:

Ask yourself: 'Do I need additional support? (for example, do you need to bring in a specialist to supervise any aspects of your project?)

Action:

Specify what you intend to do to secure the support you need (clarify availability; arrange dates for feedback and monitoring schedule).

CORRIE TEN BOOM 1892–1983

Corrie was born in Holland and grew up to be the first woman in Holland to qualify as a watchmaker. When the Germans invaded her country in 1940, she worked with the Dutch underground resistance movement. She was arrested with her family including her father, who died 10 days later. She was sent with her sister to a concentration camp until 1944. Her sister had died a few days before her release. She spent the rest of her life doing rehabilitation work for survivors and lecturing on the Holocaust. She was honoured by the State of Israel, and a film (*The Hiding Place*) was made of her life.

GUIDELINES FOR DECISION MAKING

These guidelines will help you to make a decision more easily because they encourage you to use both your right brain and left brain and your feelings in the process.

Example of Problem: cannot decide whether or not to move house after a divorce.

1   Brainstorm – put one word in the centre of a page to represent the issue about which you want to make a decision (e.g. Move – for a decision about whether or not to move house).

2   Think about all the different issues which are involved in this decision, and quickly note them anywhere on the page without thinking about them anymore (e.g. location; money; schools; view; access to work; comfort; parents; social life, etc.). The idea of this first stage is to get as many freely associated words on the paper as possible.

3   When your ideas have dried up, take a coloured pen and circle six to ten of the most key issues.

4   Take another piece of paper and head it with one of your choices (e.g. Move now); divide it into four columns. List your key issues in the first column.

5   In the second column, enter a grading for each on a scale of 1–10 according to *current* importance to *you* in terms of your needs.

6   In the third column, grade it again on a 1–10 scale in relation to its 'feel-good' factor. In other words, this is the column where you can let your heart, and not your head, be your guide!

7   In the fourth column, enter a grading which is relevant to your long-term key goals. (If you don't know what these are, turn to the section on page 78 on Spiritual Fitness.)

8   Repeat steps 4–7 for each of the choices you are able to identify (e.g. don't move until children have left school/move when we have saved ..., etc.).

9   Take a relaxing break for at least 20 minutes or so. Do something which nurtures you and helps you to forget your decision-making (e.g. have a delicious lunch; listen to some music; take a novel to the bath, etc.). If you can, as Grandma would have said, sleep on it.

10   Return to your lists, read and reflect for a *few* minutes and MAKE YOUR DECISION!

11   Make a contingency plan. This will help you to stop using any more energy on wondering whether you have made the right choice or not!

12   Celebrate with a treat (yes, another one!) and remind yourself that you are now a Thriver, and that even if your choice proves to be wrong, you will find a way of making a success out of the setback.

GOAL-SETTING – AIM FOR THE STARS

This is a strategy for achievable goal-setting in the wake of a setback.

After a setback it is very important to set new goals. There are two main reasons for doing this. The first is that the setback may have changed some of our circumstances and possibilities. The second is that we often need a motivational boost, and setting goals is very energizing.

STARS is a reminder mnemonic of the five key points we need to bear in mind when we set goals. Goals should *always* be **S**pecific, **T**ime-tabled, **A**chievable, **R**ewarded and **S**upported. The questions are to help you modify your normal goal-setting in the aftermath of a setback.

Is It Specific Enough?

Make sure that your goal is not too general, otherwise it will be difficult to measure whether or not you are making progress towards it. Good intentions and grandiose resolutions often flow freely in the emotional aftermath of a setback. We need to tame and harness these if we want them to be useful and successful. We must aim to bring them 'down to earth' by defining precisely what we are aiming to achieve.

For example, let's imagine that you missed an important appointment because you couldn't find your car keys and you declared, 'I'll be much tidier from now on.' If you want to do more than merely massage your guilt after your setback, you could turn this over-generalized 'good intention' into a STARS goal by saying: 'From tomorrow, I will check twice a day (before going to work and before going to bed) that my car keys have been put away in the right place.'

Has It Been Sensitively Time-tabled?

Every goal must have a target date. Goals which are too long term often become side-lined. (I need my deadlines to be tomorrow to get me going, as my editors know!) If you have an important long-term goal, after a setback make sure that you have clearly identified steps with completion dates in the *near* future. We need quick results for quick encouragement.

Is It Genuinely Achievable Now?

Anyone who is interested in personal development wants stretching goals – we know that there is little point in having a goal which is too easy. But after a setback, you may have to modify the way you set your goals until you have fully recovered. This is the time for dipping your toe into new waters, rather than taking a headlong dive. But remember the water should be still cold enough to be bracing! Check also that your goal is in line with your *current* priorities. Today these may be emotional healing from a hurt, and mending the garden gate. Climbing Mount Everest may be more achievable tomorrow!

How Will I Reward Myself?

No goal should ever be set without a clearly stated reward being allocated to it. After a setback, you must be particularly careful on this score and make sure that you reward *effort* as well as achievement. Don't forget that we often don't function at our best after a setback, and we may not know what our new potential is until we have tried and failed to meet our usual standard.

On Whom Will I Draw for Support?

All goals are more likely to be achieved if we publicly declare them, and someone else supports us by keeping an eye on our progress. (You can do this by telling someone verbally, or writing down your goals and pinning them up in a prominent place.)

But as our morale may well be fragile after a setback, the people supporting us must be chosen with care. They must be:

- genuinely interested in our success (and not recruited from the 'I told you so' brigade)
- honest and assertive (we need sensitively administered, straight feedback and meticulous monitoring, not 'tea and sympathy').

A STRATEGY FOR BEING PROACTIVE

The word 'PROACT' is a mnemonic reminder. Each of its letters reminds us of the following six steps we need to take to be successfully proactive.

Prepare

- Take time to think hard before acting.
- Do as much research as you can to see if what you want to do has been tried before.
- Reflect on other options.
- Script any 'speeches' you may need to make to open up discussion or argue your case.

Rest

Proactivity requires energy – the more you can have the better. Even if you are excited or there is an urgency, try to stop at this point and do something which will recharge you.

Organize

- Reschedule your diary (proactivity requires that *extra* time is 'made' for it).
- Delegate some of your tasks if necessary (this will 'buy' you extra time and energy).
- Cost and research resources required (materials, money and energy!).
- Request or negotiate support and feedback for yourself and your project.

Act

Make an action plan. Make sure it is a step-by-step one, and ensure that each goal is a STAR (as above) and get started as soon as you can.

Calculate

- Stand back and reflect objectively on progress as soon as you have completed your first few steps.
- Ask for feedback (using the guidelines above, of course!).
- Assess the budget and other relevant statistics.
- Revise your action plan if necessary.

Try Again

- Don't give up until you have tried *several* or many times.
- Each time you fail, review your goal and start the Proact strategy again!

But of course, don't beat your head until it bursts against a solid wall!

> If at first you don't succeed, try, try again. Then quit. There's no use being a damn fool about it.
>
> W. C. FIELDS

THOMAS ALVA EDISON 1847–1931

Edison's first setback occurred when he started school. He was considered stupid by his teachers because he was continually asking questions. He had to leave after three months and was educated from then on by his mother. As an inventor, his life was a continuous triumph over setback after setback when experiments failed or were rejected. He also had to struggle with bouts of serious illness and deafness caused by an accident. But by the time he died, he had patented no less than 1,093 inventions.

DEFUSING CONFLICT IN A TEAM, GROUP OR FAMILY

During the 'heat' of a setback, people who are generally sociable and sensitive can start being 'difficult' when they are in a group situation. It is human nature to look for someone to blame or to soak up one's irritation and hurt. This can be very frustrating if you are trying to make them work more co-operatively together so they can make a necessary decision (e.g. 'Now this has happened, where do we go from here?'). Try using the steps of this strategy as a guide before you walk out in despair!

To illustrate how to put it into practice, I have given some examples (in brackets). These relate to the strategy being used by a team leader at a staff meeting after a key member had recently resigned.

Don't forget that the strategy can be adapted to many other situations. You could try applying it to a family discussion that might occur following the news that Grandma is being discharged from hospital and she can no longer live at home. The problem is: Who is going to have her for the month until a nursing home is found? Everyone has other plans for their immediate life, and each feels they have done more of their fair share in looking after Mum!

The reminder mnemonic sentence is:

| **S** top | **E** veryone's | **R** acing | **P** ulses | **C** ausing | **D** isaster |
| **S** top | **E** mpathize | **R** eview | **P** rice | **C** hoices | **D** ecision |

Stop

- Interrupt any discussion calmly but firmly ('Please stop talking for a moment').
- Use appropriate assertive body language to reinforce the verbal message (putting your hand up, or even [if all else fails] some fist-banging on the table – plus direct eye contact and upright posture, of course).
- Insist that the conflict is put on hold for a moment (just keep on repeating a simple sentence such as 'We need to stop arguing now and make a decision').

Empathize

- Acknowledge the feelings of all parties. This is important because the main motivation behind many arguments on these kinds of occasions is simply to have one's feelings acknowledged ('I can see that some people are feeling depressed by the situation and a few are feeling quite angry').
- Indicate your awareness of their difficulties and problems ('I appreciate how difficult it is to have to pick up the pieces of someone else's mess as well as doing your own work').

Review

- Summarize what you yourself have noticed happening or have been told is happening ('I have noticed that John's work is just not being done').
- Use objective, non-emotive language.
- Be as specific as you can (dates, times and names if known).
- Resist generalizations and guesswork ('No one seems to care' or 'You're probably thinking that if you don't do it someone else will').

Price

- Spell out the price that will be paid individually and collectively if the conflict continues ('We will not reach our team target and we will all lose our bonuses').
- Resist exaggeration ('We'll all end up getting the sack').
- Avoid threats at this stage, even if they are appropriate ('Someone's head is going to roll sooner or later'). In the heat of the moment this kind of talk will merely put people on the defensive and may stop them taking responsibility.

Choices

- Point out (or encourage the others to look for) the alternative ways forward ('We could start a rota to cover John's work for the next month', or 'We could use some of next month's budget to employ a temp. Perhaps you might have other ideas').
- Affirm that the choice is their responsibility ('We are all affected by this setback, and so I believe we should reach a decision together').

Decision

- Give them a time-frame for making a decision from among the various alternatives ('We must have a plan in place by next Monday').
- Suggest a neutral place to meet for further discussion if necessary or appropriate ('We could meet after work in the social club for half an hour when everyone has had time to think').
- Suggest a structure for the discussion and decision-making ('Each of us could take a minute of uninterrupted time to put forward a view, and then we could take a vote').
- Point out that if they do not make a decision, one will be made by you, or the matter will be referred on ('If we don't get this sorted ourselves, I will have to put the problem to Bill Jones').

JOINT PROBLEM-SOLVING STRATEGY

Mnemonic sentence:

Collective	**P**roblem	**S**olving	**O**pens
Climate	**P**erception	**S**haring	**O**wnership
Communication	**S**o	**P**eople	**M**ellow
Causes	**S**olutions	**P**lan	**M**onitoring

Climate

Call a 'meeting' and start it by looking relaxed and using a positive energetic tone of voice. State that you expect a solution and that everyone will learn something useful from the experience.

Perception

Outline the problem caused by the setback as *you* perceive it.

Sharing

Ask each person, in turn, to state (without interruption) *their* views and perceptions.

Ownership

Decide whose problem it is and who is responsible for solving it. At this stage anyone who is not responsible could be invited to leave the 'meeting'.

Causes

List all possible causes and then highlight the most likely ones.

Solutions

Use brainstorming to elicit as many ideas as you can without judging them. When the ideas have dried up, look at the pros and cons of each one and choose one to try.

Plan

Set step-by-step goals (use the Positive Action Strategy on page 165) and assign individual tasks.

Monitoring

Decide how, and by whom, your progress will be monitored.

MICHAEL MARKS

Michael Marks was a Jewish refugee from Russia who settled in England. His first venture into the retail trade was to start a market stall in Leeds in 1884. As he was so poor, he could not afford expensive stock so he traded on the slogan 'Don't ask the price. It's a penny.' He was so successful that he took on a partner, Tom Spencer. Through perseverance and guts, they progressed their business to become the most famous British chain store, Marks & Spencer.

Mind Fitness

MAINTAINING A POSITIVE THINKING MODE

After a setback it is easy to slip into negative thinking patterns without even realizing that we have done so. Use this strategy to check that your mind is in its positive thinking mode. Teach it to others so that they can keep an eye on you as well!

The GEE Strategy

Challenge your negative thinking mood by asking yourself these three questions:

1   Am I *Generalizing* from a specific occurrence?
2   Am I *Exaggerating* the problem?
3   Am I *Excluding* the positive potential in this situation?

Repeat six times three affirmations using an appropriate tone of voice and varying the word on which you put your emphasis, such as: *I **am** calm and I am in control; I am **excited** and I want to do this.*

Here are a few suggestions which work either by diverting your mind or switching it into right-brain mode.

- Count even numbers backwards from 50 – in French or Chinese if you find English too easy!
- Draw a mandala and stare at its centre for a few minutes. (A mandala is a design used for meditation, often seen in church windows or Islamic tiles. The design is set in a circle with patterns which lead the eye to its central point.) Our brain cannot be used for worrying at the same time as it is being used to look at a mandala, or do any other kind of meditation.
- Divert your attention by focusing it on a photo of a loved one. Smile and silently tell them why you love them. Draw a bunch of flowers and then imagine yourself giving them to someone who has recently been good to you, or has done something you have admired.
- Focus your eye on one object in the room and examine it in the greatest detail – try to imagine it being used in other ways – allow yourself the freedom to see both weird and wonderful images.
- Visualize a favourite room of yours and take yourself on an imaginary tour – looking in its every corner and feeling some of its textures and shapes.
- Instead of moaning about your situation, imagine what your favourite comedian might say about it.
- Read a motivational poem.

Self-Motivation

Make your own colourful posters for motivational poems or sayings, and keep them in a handy place such as:

- the front of your diary
- inside the lid of your briefcase
- in the glove compartment of your car
- on the wall by the bath
- at the top of the stairs.

If

If you think you are beaten, you are
If you think you dare not, you don't
If you'd like to win, but think you can't
It's almost certain you won't
If you think you'll lose, you've lost
For out of the world we find
Success begins with a fellow's will
It's all in the state of mind.
If you think you're outclassed, you are
You've got to think high to rise
You've got to be sure of yourself before
You can ever win a prize.
Life's battles don't always go
To the stronger or faster man
But sooner or later the man who wins
Is the one who Thinks he can.

ANON

Don't Give Up

When things go wrong as they sometimes will,
When the road you're trudging seems uphill,
When the funds are low and the debts are high
And you want to smile but have to sigh
When care is pressing you down a bit
Rest, if you must, but don't quit
Life is queer with its twists and turns,
As every one of us sometimes learns
And many a failure turns about
When he might have won had he stuck it out

Don't give up though the pace seems slow
You may succeed with another blow
Success is failure turned inside out
The silver tint of the cloud of doubt
And you never can tell how close you are
It may be near when it seems so far.
So stick to the fight when you're hardest hit
It's when things seem worst
You must not quit

ANON

Personality Drivers of Successfully Self-motivated People

This is another bit of inspiration for you. Read it whenever any of these 36 'personality drivers' is flagging.

1 **Visionary Thinking** – without idle dreaming
2 **Unashamed Neediness** – without selfish greediness
3 **Eternal Optimism** – without denying common sense
4 **Guru-worshipping** – without blind following
5 **Sound Self-esteem** – without ignorant arrogance
6 **Thirst for Challenge** – without scorning easy options
7 **Addiction to Achievement** – without imprudent impatience
8 **Steadfast Principles** – without narrow prejudice
9 **Consistent Courage** – without thoughtless gambling
10 **Endless energy** – without debilitating burnout
11 **Prepared Proactivity** – without disregard for opportunity
12 **Solid responsibility** – without rigid perfectionism
13 **Calm concentration** – without repressed creativity
14 **Systematic Organization** – without obtuse obsessionality
15 **Meticulous Planning** – without stubborn inflexibility
16 **Sharp Decisiveness** – without blindness to consequence
17 **Slick presentation** – without enslavement to fashion
18 **Positive Problem-solving** – without immunity to despair
19 **Reliable intuition** – without acting on every hunch
20 **Searching Self-reflection** – without frustrating self-absorption

21 **Pride in individuality** – without disregard for human commonality
22 **Deep emotionality** – without enslavement to feelings
23 **Stringent Self-criticism** – without suffocating self-abuse
24 **Intolerance of excuses** – without deafness to their message
25 **Sincere Self-forgiveness** – without self-inflicted punishment
26 **Personal Power** – without disempowering others
27 **Assertive Directness** – without thoughtless insensitivity
28 **Skilled Self-protection** – without harmful aggression
29 **Perpetual Learning** – without devaluing own wisdom
30 **Serious Focus** – without humourless solemnity
31 **Sensible Self-nurturing** – without spurning support
32 **Seeker of Solitude** – without reclusive aloofness
33 **Reveller in Success** – without fear of failure
34 **Scrupulous Self-healing** – without dismissing comfort
35 **Ample Self-reward** – without rejecting recognition
36 **Inward Drive** – without scorning incentives

An explanation of how these Drivers work and how you can develop them can be found in my book *Self Motivation.*

BRAIN GYM

The following simple physical exercises will stimulate your thinking brain and enable you to switch much more easily from right- and left-brain mode. The exercises were first developed to help children with dyslexia, so they will be particularly helpful if, like me, you suffer with that kind of learning difficulty. If these exercises are done regularly, new nerve networks are formed between the two hemispheres.

The Cross Crawl

This involves simply walking slowly for a few minutes, on the spot, while touching your knee with the opposite elbow as it is raised for each pace.

Brain Buttons

Place one hand on your navel. With the thumb and second finger of the other, find the two indentations between the first and second ribs directly under the collar bone, to the right and left of the sternum. The latter position is where blood flows directly to the brain. The exercise simply involves holding one hand on the navel while gently massaging in these indentations.

Brainstorming

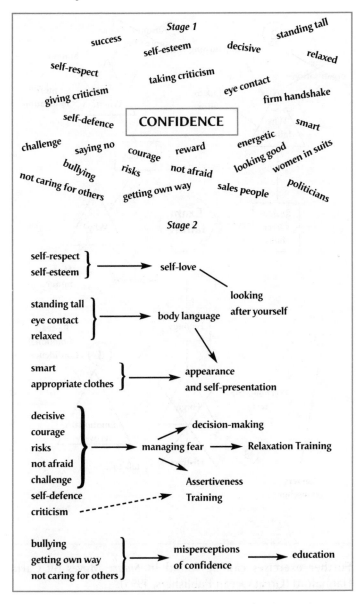

Stage 1

success
self-esteem
decisive
standing tall
relaxed
self-respect
taking criticism
giving criticism
eye contact
firm handshake
self-defence

CONFIDENCE

smart
challenge
saying no
courage
reward
energetic
looking good
women in suits
bullying
risks
not afraid
not caring for others
getting own way
sales people
politicians

Stage 2

self-respect
self-esteem } → self-love
looking
after yourself

standing tall
eye contact → body language
relaxed

smart
appropriate clothes } → appearance
and self-presentation

decisive
courage
risks
not afraid
challenge
self-defence
criticism } → managing fear → decision-making
→ Relaxation Training
→ Assertiveness
Training

bullying
getting own way
not caring for others } → misperceptions
of confidence → education

183

Mind Map

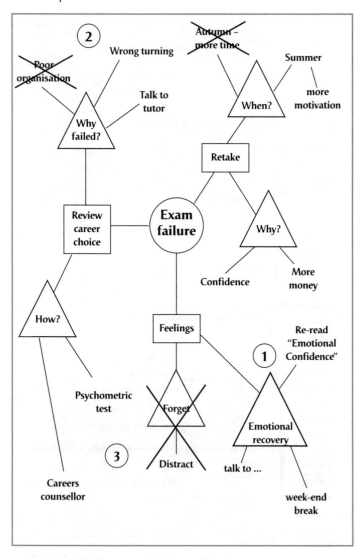

Further exercises can be found in *Smart Moves* by Carla Hannaford (Great Ocean Publishers, 1995).

The Way

Forward

I hope that you have enjoyed reading this book and that it will continue to be a useful tool to help you through all manner of setbacks. I have found it an inspiring book to write and would be most interested to know if it has been interesting and helpful to read for you. You can contact me via my website:
www.gael-lindenfield.com

Good luck on your journey through life!

Further

Reading

A Guided Tour of My Own Books That Contain Relevant Information and Advice

ASSERT YOURSELF

An introduction to the theory behind Assertiveness Training. Includes advice, strategies and exercises on the following:

- making persistent requests
- negotiation
- dealing with put-downs
- criticism.

It also includes a section on how to run your own self-help group and do effective role-plays.

SUPER CONFIDENCE

This book was originally written for women but is now widely used by men as well. It includes:

- explanation of the difference between inner and outer confidence
- hallmarks of a confident person
- exercises to improve self-knowledge (including the effect of your childhood and your values)
- overview of transactional analysis personality theory
- guidelines on confident communication.

THE POSITIVE WOMAN

- how to break negative habits of thinking, feeling and behaviour
- how to improve your physical well-being
- revitalizing your personal relationships
- giving your lifestyle a management boost.

MANAGING ANGER

- explanation of how anger works and how our anger responses develop
- the difference between aggressive, passive and assertive styles of expressing anger
- exercise on identifying your own anger patterns
- how to deal with a backlog of anger
- how to express anger safely and constructively
- how to respond to others' anger
- strategy for channelling surplus anger energy into constructive projects.

SELF ESTEEM

- overview of the elements of self-esteem and how it is developed and diminished
- strategy for breaking self-sabotaging habits

- strategy for healing emotional wounds that have damaged self-esteem
- self-help programme for reconditioning self esteem which has been at a low ebb for many years
- strategy for regular maintenance of healthy self-esteem
- advice on how to recover from a 'crash' in self-esteem after a crisis
- how to build esteem of others at work and at home.

SELF MOTIVATION

Instant self-help exercises and guidelines designed to build or boost the 36 paradoxical character traits driving self-motivated people. For example:

- Driver 1: visionary thinking without idle dreaming
- Driver 4: guru-worshipping without blind following
- Driver 9: consistent courage without thoughtless gambling
- Driver 13: calm concentration without repressed creativity
- Driver 20: stringent self-criticism without self-abuse
- Driver 26: personal power without disempowering others
- Driver 36: inwardly driven without scorning incentives.

Also contains inspirational chapter on favourite quick-fixes after a setback from highly self-motivated people.

EMOTIONAL CONFIDENCE

- explanation of how our emotional system operates
- keys to building confidence in your ability to take control of your own emotions
- seven-step strategy for healing emotional hurt
- strategies and tips on handling runaway feelings such as guilt, jealousy, anger and apathy
- how to maintain emotional confidence.

CONFIDENT CHILDREN

A self-help programme for parents to enable them to :

- understand their own conditioned parental responses
- build children's self-esteem
- teach children relevant social skills
- provide a confidence-building environment and family strategies for problem-solving and dealing with conflict.

POSITIVE UNDER PRESSURE

This book was jointly written with a physician colleague, Dr Malcolm VandenBurg. It is based upon a highly successful series of workshops that were originally designed to help high-achieving people in the business and professional worlds to harness the positive power of their pressure. This book is a self-help version of the programme. It can be used by anyone who wants to avoid the pitfalls of stress that living a hectic, fast-paced life can bring. It will teach you how to:

- understand and control your early warning signs of stress
- say 'No' to pressure you do not need or want
- think positively
- relax yourself wherever you are.

BOOKS ON TAPE

The following books are available on cassette:

- *Self Motivation*
- *Self Esteem*
- *Emotional Confidence*
- *Success from Setbacks*

MANAGING EMOTIONS AT WORK

This is a special cassette designed mainly for use at work. It contains a range of quick-fix strategies to help you take control of feelings that may be inhibiting you from doing what you want or need to do (e.g. over-anxiety, anger and frustration, dislike and apathy).

A selection of books by other authors

EMOTIONAL SKILLS

Daniel Goleman, *Emotional Intelligence* (Bantam, 1995)
Dr Kenneth Hambly, *Banish Anxiety* (Thorsons, 1991)
Susan Jeffers, *Feel the Fear and Do It Anyway* (Arrow, 1987)
Dorothy Rowe, *Beyond Fear* (Fontana, 1987)
Paul Wilson *The Little Book of Calm* and *The Calm Technique*
(Thorsons, 1997)

ORGANIZATIONAL SKILLS

Stephen Covey, *The Seven Habits of Highly Effective People*
(Simon and Schuster, 1989)
Roger Dawson, *The Confident Decision Maker*
Wess Roberts, *Leadership Secrets of Attila the Hun*

MIND FITNESS

Edward de Bono, *I Am Right You Are Wrong* (Penguin, 1991)
Tony Buzan, *Make the Most of Your Mind* (Pan, 1988)
Alan Carmichael, *Believe You Can* (Concept, 1991)
Patricia Carrington, *The Book of Meditation* (Element, 1998)
Susan Greenfield *The Human Brain* (Phoenix, 1997)
Carla Hannaford, *Smart Moves* (Great Ocean, 1995)
Vera Peiffer, *Positive Thinking* (Element, 1989)

HELPING OTHERS

Susan Quilliam, *What to Do When You Really Want to Help Someone But Don't Know How* (Transformation Press, 1998)

SPIRITUAL FITNESS

James Hillman, *The Soul's Code* (Bantam, 1996)
Thomas Moore, *The Re-enchantment of Everyday Life* (Hodder and Stoughton, 1996)

GENERAL MOTIVATION

Robert Holden, *Living Wonderfully* (Thorsons, 1994)
David McNally, *Even Eagles Need a Push* (Thorsons, 1993)
Glenys Parry, *Coping With Crises* (BPS Books, 1990)
Arthur Pine, *When One Door Closes, Another Opens* (Dell, 1993)
Dr Al Siebart, *How to Survive in Any Life Crisis* (Thorsons, 1993)
Anthony Robbins, *Awaken the Giant Within* (Simon and Schuster, 1992)

INSPIRATION

Read any autobiography or biography on any of the people whose stories I have summarized in this book.

Index